T0302233

ANTI-BURNOUT

Burnout results in people feeling exhausted, cynical, detached and hopeless – even depressed and anxious. This book looks at burnout from an individual, group and organisational perspective. It uses anecdotes from the author's life; and examples from literature, poetry and art to bring the subject to life. Based on the latest scientific thinking on burnout and evidence-based ideas, this practical, easy read book gives leaders the knowledge they need to create a psychologically healthy and high performance culture at work.

After reading this book, you will understand more about burnout than 90 per cent of the population. You will know what to do to prevent burnout in other people and in yourself. *Anti-burnout* is an academically rigorous book, written in a friendly, engaging, conversational style. It contains lots of anecdotes, examples from the arts and stories that illustrate and bring to life the practical advice on preventing burnout. *Anti-burnout* will answer these questions:

- What exactly is burnout?
- How does burnout affect individuals, teams and organisations?
- What causes burnout?
- How can I understand and support people with burnout?
- How can I prevent myself from burning out?
- What are the obstacles to preventing burnout?
- How does remote working affect burnout?
- What can I do to create a workplace culture that prevents burnout?

This book is helpful because it relates the scientific literature on burnout to real life. *Anti-burnout* looks at the individual factors in burnout, including personality and mental health. It also looks at how the dynamics of teams and how work is organised relate to burnout. Finally, the book investigates organisational culture, leadership and burnout. This book is essential reading for leaders and managers who want to minimise burnout in people in their organisation. It will also be essential reading for anyone with an interest in mental well-being at work such as occupational health practitioners, researchers and human resource professionals.

Michael Drayton is an executive coach, organisational consultant and clinical psychologist. He is an expert in leadership, resilience and mental health at work. Mike was educated at LSE, Oxford Saïd Business School and the University of Birmingham.

ANTI-BURNOUT

How to Create a Psychologically Safe and High-performance Organisation

Michael Drayton

Routledge
Taylor & Francis Group

LONDON AND NEW YORK

First published 2021
by Routledge
2 Park Square, Milton Park, Abingdon, Oxon OX14 4RN

and by Routledge
52 Vanderbilt Avenue, New York, NY 10017

Routledge is an imprint of the Taylor & Francis Group, an informa business

British Library Cataloguing-in-Publication Data
A catalogue record for this book is available from the British Library

Library of Congress Cataloging-in-Publication Data
Names: Drayton, Michael, 1960– author.
Title: Anti-burnout : how to create a psychologically safe and high-performance organisation / Michael Drayton.
Description: Milton Park, Abingdon, Oxon;
New York, NY : Routledge, 2021. |
Includes bibliographical references and index. |
Identifiers: LCCN 2020038757 (print) |
LCCN 2020038758 (ebook) | ISBN 9780367460532 (hardback) |
ISBN 9781003027157 (ebook)
Subjects: LCSH: Burn out (Psychology) |
Job stress. | Psychology, Industrial.
Classification: LCC BF481 .D73 2021 (print) |
LCC BF481 (ebook) | DDC 158.7/23—dc23
LC record available at https://lccn.loc.gov/2020038757
LC ebook record available at https://lccn.loc.gov/2020038758

ISBN: 978-0-367-46053-2 (hbk)
ISBN: 978-0-367-69818-8 (pbk)
ISBN: 978-1-003-02715-7 (ebk)

Typeset in Joanna
by codeMantra

CONTENTS

Section 3: Organisation

ILLUSTRATIONS

Figures

Table

ABOUT THE AUTHOR

Dr Mike Drayton is an executive coach, organisational consultant and clinical psychologist. He has over 20 years' experience in mental well-being in the workplace. His clients include: a world-famous Japanese consumer electronics company, a Swiss owned multinational pharmaceuticals company, a European rail company and the Cabinet Office. Mike is also unique in that he has lived experience of work-related mental health problems. In the 1980s he worked as a paramedic and attended the Clapham Rail Disaster. As a result, he developed PTSD. Mike describes his experiences in the book. Mike was educated at LSE, the University of Oxford, and the University of Birmingham. Mike is a Fellow of the Cabinet Office Emergency Planning College. He is a clinical psychologist licensed with the Health and Care Professions Council (HCPC) and an Executive Coach accredited at Senior Practitioner level by the European Mentoring and Coaching Council (EMCC). He is a Chartered Psychologist and an Associate fellow of the British Psychological Society.

INTRODUCTION

Have you ever felt so tired that you couldn't think? Have you ever felt really exhausted, but at the same time unable to switch off, relax or even sleep? Do you ever feel cynical about your job and wonder what the point of it all is? If you have experienced any of the above, you may be on the road to burnout.

This is a book about burnout – the biggest public health crisis of the 21st century. Burnout is a visceral physical experience. It's the exhaustion, the anxiety, the sick feeling in your stomach. Burnout is also in your head. It's the cynicism, negativity and detachment from work and people. It's the inability to think clearly, the absence of mental well-being. People on the road to burnout are often clinically anxious and depressed.

Personality plays a role in burnout. Conscientious people are more likely to suffer burnout than those who are low on this personality factor. But why burn out? The roots of burnout are in a toxic organisational culture. Burnout is also a social and political experience, because it happens in the context of an organisational culture, which in turn exists in an economy.

Economic uncertainty impacts on organisational culture, and this can find expression in staff burnout.

As well as the personal, public health and humanitarian effects, there's a massive financial price. Burnout costs British companies a fortune in high levels of sickness and employee absence, along with poor retention and poor performance due to presenteeism (HSE, 2019).

This isn't right! Work shouldn't make people ill. In fact, I believe the opposite should be true: work should promote good mental health by giving people purpose, meaning and connection with others.

One of the obstacles to addressing burnout is that organisations tend to treat it as an individual or personal problem rather than a broader organisational challenge. To minimise burnout, it has to be seen as a systemic issue needing board-level action.

This is a book for leaders and managers, and also for those on the road to burnout or recovering from burnout. It's a practical book that will give you the latest scientific thinking on burnout and evidence-based ideas about how to make things better for individuals and for organisations. This book will help you to become part of the solution, not the problem.

This book is a manifesto, a call to action for leaders, managers and anyone who has had that experience of 'vital exhaustion'. It's a book for those who want to create a positive, psychologically healthy culture at work.

What does this book cover?

Section 1: Person

This section covers the individual factors that contribute to burnout.

Chapter 1 explores what burnout really is. I describe the experience of burnout using the World Health Organization's framework. I talk a bit about the history of burnout. I also look at the bigger picture, seeing burnout in the context of organisational culture.

Chapter 2 looks at burnout and mental health at work. I discuss the difference between normal human emotions such as worry and feeling fed-up, and clinical disorders like anxiety and depression. I give you some simple advice about distinguishing between normal emotions, which you shouldn't be concerned about, and signs of clinical depression or anxiety, which should worry you. I end by talking about the importance of energy in managing burnout.

Chapter 3 is all about burnout and personality. I explain how psychologists understand personality using a model called the 'Big Five'. Some personality types are more susceptible to burnout than others, and if you are vulnerable, you'll find guidance in this chapter on how you can protect yourself. I also touch on the idea of personality disorder burnout and mental well-being. To finish up, I talk about men and women – how gender influences the way in which we manage stress and burnout.

In Chapter 4, I look at why it seems so hard to address burnout and poor mental well-being in ourselves and in other people. I tell you about research from the fields of social psychology, neuroscience and cognitive science that can help us to understand and break down the barriers to managing stress and burnout.

Section 2: Role

This section is all about your job and your day-to-day life at work. I share practical steps you can take to protect yourself, and those you manage, from going down the road to burnout.

Chapter 5 is about the psychology of office politics. It explains some ideas and practical tools for understanding and managing the dynamics of the group of people you work with.

Chapter 6 focuses on you – on how you can look after your own well-being whilst you are at work. The key to this is not so much managing your time or workload, but managing your energy levels.

Chapter 7 is about how you can protect the people you manage from burnout. I revisit how you can spot the early-warning signs of burnout. I highlight the importance of communication and talking to people who might be struggling. Finally, I tell you about some simple and straightforward techniques that you can introduce to change the culture of the group of people with whom you work directly.

Section 3: Organisation

Section 3 zooms out to examine the wider organisational and social system in which burnout happens.

Chapter 8 looks at the role that organisational culture plays in burnout. By far the biggest factor in burnout is a toxic workplace culture. What kind of day-to-day experiences do people in your organisation have? It is these millions of experiences that form either a positive or toxic organisational culture. I discuss practical initiatives you can introduce (like encouraging a thinking environment) that create a positive culture at work.

Chapter 9 is about leadership. Organisations are reflections of their leaders. This chapter examines the crucial role of proactive leadership in creating a psychologically healthy and high-performance culture. Gandhi famously said, "Be the change that you wish to see in the world." Leaders should embody psychological safety in their own lives and model psychologically healthy attitudes and behaviour to those they lead.

Chapter 10 is all about how you can make this happen, both personally and organisationally. I draw together all the themes in the book and present them as a framework that you can adapt to your life, your job and your organisation.

Everything I suggest in this book is common sense. However, as we all know, common sense is one of the rarest commodities in this world. Everything I suggest is simple to know but hard to do. But as a leader you are paid to do hard stuff, and it is the hard things that bring meaning and satisfaction. What is more important than creating a psychologically safe and high-performance workplace environment?

Reference

HSE (2019). *Work-related Stress, Anxiety or Depression Statistics in Great Britain, 2019*. London: HSE.

Section 1

PERSON

1

WHAT IS BURNOUT?

Pause for a moment and think about burnout. What image comes to mind? Is it a frazzled man or woman who is agitated and not coping? Is the person running around trying to keep up, or maybe sitting at a desk in front of a computer looking exhausted and defeated?

Burnout is all of these things and a whole lot more. When most people are asked to consider burnout, they think of it as being synonymous with overwork. They might explain burnout as exhaustion caused by too much work. However, exhaustion is only one part of the burnout jigsaw. Other pieces include psychological and spiritual factors like cynicism, hopelessness and helplessness, and detachment – not only from work but from life. These psychological, emotional and spiritual aspects of burnout are a lot more damaging to people than the physical exhaustion.

The writer Sam Keen described burnout thus: "Burnout is nature's way of telling you, you've been going through the motions, your soul has departed; you're a zombie, a member of the walking dead, a sleepwalker. False optimism is like administering stimulants to an exhausted nervous system." (Keen, 1992)

I won't be offering any false optimism in this book. I will explain the science behind burnout and provide some practical suggestions to remedy it.

BOX 1.1 THE HISTORY OF BURNOUT

The term 'burnout' was first used in New York in the 1970s to describe how volunteers who worked with the city's population of drug addicts were emotionally affected by their work. The term was coined by the American psychologist Herbert Freudenberger, who helped to develop the free clinic movement in New York to support people suffering from addictions. Freudenberger, who devoted a large amount of time to these clinics, without pay, observed the gradual emotional exhaustion and declining motivation in some clinic volunteers, and termed this phenomenon 'burnout'. He defined it as "a state of mental and physical exhaustion caused by one's professional life" (Freudenberger, 1975). Jobs can be exhausting for lots of different reasons. Some people do jobs that are tedious, lack meaning and are badly paid. Others do very emotionally demanding jobs, working with people in pain (like the New York drug workers in Freudenberger's clinic). Some do jobs where the demands far outstrip the resources, and others work for employers who treat them badly. Whatever the situation, people can't simply absorb these stresses. They manifest in physical exhaustion, cynicism, detachment from the work and greatly reduced performance.

Why understanding burnout is important for you

There are three reasons why it is important for you to understand burnout, whether you are a leader, a busy manager or work for an organisation:

- Having a good understanding of how and why burnout occurs might prevent you from burning out.
- If you are a manager and you have a direct report who's at risk of burnout or is suffering with burnout, then it's important to know what you're dealing with and how you can best help.
- If you are a leader in an organisation, then understanding burnout will help you to develop an organisational culture where burnout is a thing of the past. This will translate into a highly engaged workforce and a high-performance, creative and generally happy organisational culture.

In this chapter, I describe in detail what burnout is; and believe me, it isn't very pleasant, let alone optimistic. It makes for grim reading. But at the end, you will know more about burnout than 99 per cent of the population. You will know and understand your enemy – and burnout is your enemy.

Once you understand the problem and how complex it is, we can start to come up with some solutions.

Many years ago, I trained as a clinical psychologist. One of the first things that gets drummed into you in training is that when a person turns up for help with a problem (let's say depression), you have to really understand the problem, the person and that person's life before rushing into treatment. Often, when treatment fails it's because the psychologist hasn't taken the time to really understand the factors that constitute the problem. Maybe they've taken a cookbook approach, thinking that the treatment for depression with the best evidence base is cognitive behavioural therapy, and so that's what the person got. But what if the person's depression was the result of unspeakable childhood trauma or a head injury which they didn't think was relevant and didn't disclose? Then all the CBT in the world ain't gonna help. Similarly, burnout is usually addressed like this, with off-the-peg cookbook solutions that more often than not fail to have any impact whatsoever.

So before we rush into solutions, let's spend a bit of time trying to really understand the problem of burnout.

Burnout: the World Health Organization gets involved

In 2018, the World Health Organization (WHO) included burnout in the *International Classification of Diseases* (11th Revision; ICD-11), in the section entitled 'Mental and Behavioural Disorders' (World Health Organization, 2018).

What is ICD-11?

ICD-11 is a book that clinicians use to diagnose mental health problems. It contains detailed descriptions of mental illnesses, and lists of signs and symptoms (diagnostic criteria) that a person would have to meet to be diagnosed with a particular mental illness. Take depression, for example. There are three groups of symptoms that characterise a depressive episode: first, low mood; second, disturbances in physical functioning such as poor sleep and appetite; and third, problems with thinking such as poor concentration and memory. In order to be diagnosed with depression, you would need to be suffering with specific signs or symptoms from each of these groups. (I go into this in more depth in Chapter 2.) Being diagnosed with depression isn't as simple as just feeling fed-up; there's more to it than that. ICD-11 covers all mental disorders from depression right through to serious mental illnesses such as schizophrenia.

The organisational context of burnout

Burnout is included in ICD-11 as an occupational phenomenon, not as a mental illness. It's interesting to note the emphasis on 'occupational' rather than illness.

Burnout is described in the chapter 'Factors influencing health status or contact with health services'. This chapter makes the point that burnout only occurs in the context of working for an organisation, whereas other mental health problems can occur in any context.

This is important to note, because it means that employers and workplaces are necessary conditions for burnout. In other words, burnout is not just an individual phenomenon existing within an individual person. Burnout is the consequence of a dysfunctional system.

The mistake that many employers make is to locate burnout firmly within the individual and fail to see the circumstances surrounding that individual that have led to them suffering burnout. The problem, it is assumed, is a 'weak' individual who is not coping with the day-to-day stresses of work. The solutions that emerge from this wrong assumption target the individual. Often, such solutions include things like antidepressant medication. These are sometimes supplemented with psychological techniques like time-management training, mindfulness or cognitive behavioural therapy. These interventions are positive and helpful, but they are still individual solutions to a systemic problem. They only tackle one factor contributing to the problem. The other factor is the workplace environment that triggered the burnout in the first instance.

For every employee that goes off sick with burnout, there will be many others on the edge of burning out. Burnout is a symptom that something is going wrong in the organisation – an underlying organisational 'disease' that has to be diagnosed and cured. We have to help the individual suffering with burnout, and I talk about how we do this later, but the organisation also has a responsibility to address the situation that led to the burnout in the first place.

"A state of vital exhaustion"

The WHO describes burnout as "a state of vital exhaustion" (World Health Organization, 2018). I think that's a terrific (and rather poetic) description. The word 'vital' conjures up images of energy and liveliness, and of something that is absolutely essential. 'Exhaustion' is a state of extreme physical and mental tiredness, and to exhaust something means to use it up to the point where all reserves are depleted. These two words beautifully sum up the experience of burnout. The person suffering from burnout feels exhausted. They feel that their resources have been completely depleted. At the same time, the person experiences a sense of agitation and energy. They feel that they just can't switch off or relax. All the people I have met who have been suffering with burnout have experienced this combination of agitation and exhaustion.

ICD-11 goes on to describe burnout as being:

> a syndrome conceptualised as resulting from chronic workplace stress that has not been successfully managed. It is characterised by three dimensions:
>
> 1   feelings of energy depletion or exhaustion;
> 2   increased mental distance from one's job, negativism or cynicism related to one's job, and;
> 3   reduced professional efficacy.
>
> Burnout refers specifically to phenomena in the occupational context and should not be applied to describe experiences in other areas of life. (WHO, 2018)

This definition focuses squarely on the occupational context of burnout rather than the individual 'illness' context. It follows that the best way to avoid burnout and help people suffering with burnout is to focus on fixing the workplace as well as 'fixing' (helping and supporting) the individual employee. A systemic and multi-level approach to burnout is important.

Burnout is related to poorly managed stress in the environment, rather than weakness on the part of susceptible employees. Taking an individual approach to managing burnout brings to mind the experiences of shell-shocked soldiers and airmen in both World Wars. According to military psychiatrists at the time, shell shock (or PTSD as it would now be known) was a result of individual weakness rather than the hellish conditions of trench warfare or the terrible casualty rates of World War II bomber crews. Servicemen who developed shell shock would have their military records stamped with the terrible acronym 'LMF', which stands for lack of moral fibre. These soldiers were told that the cause of their shellshock wasn't the appalling environment but a weakness in their personality. That attitude persists in many organisations, where burnout is attributed to the weakness of the employee rather than the toxicity of the organisational culture and environment. This attitude adds to the distress of the individual, who sees themselves as being weak as well as burnt out. It also absolves the organisation of any blame, guilt and need to change.

BOX 1.2 ROB'S STORY

It is one a.m. and in the bedroom of a modest semi-detached house in a London suburb Rob lies next to his wife, Marie, who is quietly snoring. He is wide awake and staring into the darkness. Two hours ago he was exhausted. He couldn't keep his eyes open, let alone focus on the TV programme he was watching with Marie. Now, he can't sleep. He is worrying about work. Rob's typical pattern is to fall asleep quickly and then wake up a few hours later with a feeling of panic.

He decides to get up, thinking that he may as well be working rather than just not sleeping. He swings his legs out of bed, puts on his slippers and dressing gown, and tiptoes quietly downstairs to the kitchen. He pours himself a large whisky and switches on his laptop, which he's left open on the kitchen table, and begins work.

Rob is the in-house solicitor and company secretary of a global professional services firm. The firm is in the middle of a multimillion-pound piece of litigation, which Rob is leading. He feels terrified that he has missed something, because his concentration and memory have been terrible of late.

As he stares at the screen, he hears Marie padding down the stairs. He quickly hides his drink in the cupboard over the sink. A brief argument follows, the gist of which is Marie telling Rob off for working at home. He replies along the lines of, "I know, I know." Then Marie smells the whisky and loses her temper. Rob shouts back, "Just bloody leave it, will you!" This is quickly followed by, "I'm sorry, love, I didn't..." But Marie is already climbing the stairs, sobbing. Rob goes back to the document on his laptop.

He has been a lawyer for over 20 years. After he qualified, he worked for a private practice law firm, but he didn't like the competitive business development aspects of private law. It just didn't suit his personality. So he decided to move into a general counsel role, firstly with a retail company and now with the global professional services firm. He enjoyed his job up until the last two years, when the pressures really escalated because of a combination of the uncertainty around Brexit and a merger with a rival firm. These events doubled his workload, which was big to begin with. He also had to become involved with tasks he found up-setting, like advising on redundancies. As the pressures increased, he took on more and more work. He felt sorry for the junior lawyers whom he managed and would support them by taking on their more complex tasks himself. He began to hate his job, but felt trapped.

The only way he could keep on top of things was to take work home, and this caused a lot of tension between Rob and Marie. He'd always enjoyed a couple of glasses of wine at night, but now he was having a 'nightcap' of Scotch before bed to help him sleep. His increasing alcohol consumption was another cause of conflict with his wife. The main thing that bothered him, though, was his insomnia. He just couldn't sleep, and this made his workload all the more impossible to tackle. He felt tired all the time, but also tense. *If only I could get a good night's sleep*, he would think. Sometimes Rob would daydream, and his favourite fantasy was becoming ill or breaking a leg so he wouldn't have to go to work. *God, I hate my job and I hate my life*, he would think as he lay there in the dark next to his quietly snoring wife.

A slow process

Burnout is the dramatic endpoint of a long, slow, miserable process. People aren't okay one minute and the next minute burnt out; it takes a long time to get there. This might seem obvious, but in my experience organisations and their support structures respond to burnout as if it is an all-or-nothing phenomenon. Responses to burnout are, more often than not, reactive rather than proactive. Organisations respond to the crisis, not the numerous early-warning signs. Most of us are aware when we aren't coping particularly well, and usually we notice when a colleague isn't coping. However, it's common for us to turn a blind eye to these early-warning signs of burnout and do nothing. There are many reasons for this. Later on in this book, I describe cognitive biases that can often get in the way of a proactive approach. To prevent burnout, we as individuals, managers and leaders (in other words, the people in an organisation) need to take a proactive, compassionate and systemic approach.

The burnout matrix

A matrix is the set of conditions that provides a system in which something grows or develops. That 'something' could be a high-performance workplace or it could be a workplace characterised by burnout.

To properly understand a complex phenomenon such as burnout, it's important to see it in the context of the organisation as a whole, as part of an organic system. The WHO's definition of burnout emphasises the employment context rather than the individual 'illness' context. Most organisations do the opposite, though, and see burnout as a manifestation of some kind of weakness in the employee. So most interventions to address burnout are individual, not systemic. But if we accept the WHO's hypothesis (which I do, because it is based on evidence and research), it follows that any attempt to properly understand and ameliorate burnout has to take into account systemic factors. Burnout is multifactorial. It isn't caused by just one thing, like individual weakness or a tyrannical boss, but many things that interact.

The Tavistock Institute for Human Relations was formed in 1946, to apply ideas from psychology and psychoanalysis to the problems of post war industry in the UK. The innovative work they carried out had an enormous impact on industries such as coal mining and the development of the newly formed National Health Service. Organisational consultants at the Tavistock have been wrestling with the problem of understanding complex phenomena in organisations since (Trist & Murray, 1990). They have developed a very useful model that helps us to understand organisational complexity. This model is simple but enormously helpful in that it places burnout firmly in its organisational context. This is the person/role/organisation model.

The person/role/organisation model

To reiterate, the cause of burnout is multifactorial. Burnout happens not because of individual weakness or a bad manager or overwork; it occurs when these factors and others interact with each other. The factors of burnout fall into one of three broad categories of the model:

The person

Burnout happens in individual human beings. To understand burnout it's important to understand what the individual brings to the party. All of us are complex and fallible human beings with a history of experiences from infancy that have made us the person we are. Some people are more resilient than others. Some people have personalities that make them more vulnerable to burnout than other people. If you have a personality characterised by high levels of conscientiousness and a low level of emotional stability then you are far more likely to develop burnout than someone who is laid-back and emotionally stable. If a person is suffering stress in their home life – perhaps their partner is ill or they are experiencing financial worries – then they are far more vulnerable to developing burnout than if their domestic circumstances were stable.

These individual characteristics all play a role in burnout. The problem is that many organisations, human resource departments and occupational health professionals only see these individual characteristics and miss the bigger picture – including the role that the person has to play at work and in the organisational culture.

The role

Burnout is something that occurs in an individual, but only in the context of work. People have both formal and informal roles at work, and both can contribute to burnout.

The formal role is what the person is paid to do; for example, 'head of marketing', 'engineer' or 'HR director'. One of the most common factors contributing to burnout is a lack of clarity about what the person is expected to do and achieve at work, otherwise known as role ambiguity (Peterson et al., 1995).

As well as their formal role at work, people often have informal roles, such as 'father figure', 'troublemaker', 'peacemaker' or 'scapegoat'. Our early life experiences pre-dispose us to take up these roles, and we are gently pushed into them by unconscious organisational forces (Obholzer & Roberts, 2019). These unconscious work roles can be the cause of enormous stress and contribute to burnout.

The organisation

This refers to the culture of the organisation in which the person works. It also refers to all the external pressures on that organisation from the economy, from political events and generally from the social system within which the organisation has to function.

Many organisations are psychologically very healthy and take care of their employees. Others are not so good. However, when put under pressure from economic and political circumstances, even decent organisations can soon deteriorate into toxic environments.

For example, France Télécom (or Orange SR, as it was then known) was facing an existential crisis in 2005. It was losing money hand over fist and needed to make redundancies. However, because of the strict labour laws in France, it found making people redundant to be almost impossible. It reacted by making the organisation an extremely unpleasant place to work for the people it wanted to get rid of. The CEO at the time, Didier Lombard, was famously reported to have told a meeting of managers in 2006, "I will get people to leave one way or another, either through the window or the door." Which, very tragically, is what happened. The company was hit by a wave of employee suicides that were directly attributed to the culture of bullying started by the CEO. In 2019, three executives from the company, the CEO (Lombard), his deputy and the director of human resources, were jailed because of their behaviour.

Bringing it all together

Anti-burnout is structured in-line with the three parts of the person/role/organisation model.

I describe in more detail the personal, individual factors that make people more or less vulnerable to burnout. I also talk about what individuals can do to 'inoculate' themselves to prevent burnout.

I go on to describe the role the person plays in the organisation – in other words, what their job is. I describe the job characteristics that contribute to burnout. I also outline some practical techniques you can use, again to protect yourself, but also, if you are a manager, to protect your direct reports.

The third and final section looks at organisational factors implicated in burnout. I explore organisational cultures both good and bad.

Chapter takeaways

Burnout isn't just exhaustion from overwork. It consists of:

- Feeling a mixture of physical and mental exhaustion mixed up with agitation, worry and anxiety.
- Experiencing work as being meaningless, a chore. Feeling cut off and cynical about work.
- A noticeable decline in work performance.
- Burnout isn't just an individual issue it is an organisational and wider systemic phenomenon.

To understand and prevent burnout you have to understand three factors:

- The person.
- The person's role.
- The culture of the organisation.

References

Freudenberger, H. J. (1975). 'The Staff Burn-out Syndrome'. *Special Studies – Drug Abuse Council, Inc.: SS-7.* Washington: Drug Abuse Council.

Keen, S. (1992). *Fire in the Belly: On Being a Man.* London: Piatkus.

Obholzer, A. & Roberts, V. Z. (eds) (2019). *The Unconscious at Work: A Tavistock Approach to Making Sense of Organizational Life* (2nd ed.). Abingdon: Routledge.

Peterson, M. F., Smith, P. B., Akande, A., Ayestaran, S., Bochner, S., Callan, V. ... Viedge, C. (1995). 'Role Conflict, Ambiguity, and Overload: A 21-Nation Study'. *The Academy of Management Journal*, *38*(2), 429–52.

Trist, E. & Murray, H. (1990). 'Historical Overview: The Foundation and Development of the Tavistock Institute'. In E. Trist, H. Murray & B. Trist (Eds.), *A Tavistock Anthology: The Socio-Psychological Perspective. The Social Engagement of Social Science, Volume 1* (pp. 1–34). Philadelphia, PA: University of Pennsylvania Press.

World Health Organization (2018). *International Classification of Diseases for Mortality and Morbidity Statistics (11th Revision)*. Geneva: World Health Organization.

2

BURNOUT AND MENTAL HEALTH

It's impossible to understand burnout without first understanding the basics of mental health and mental illness. This is because essentially burnout is mental ill health manifesting in an organisation.

To effectively address burnout you have to know how to recognise the signs and symptoms of mental ill health. More importantly, you need to recognise the early warning signs, so you can be proactive in not only helping others, but also yourself.

It is sometimes difficult to figure out the difference between normal human emotions, like feeling fed-up, down in the dumps or worried, and more serious clinical disorders like depression. Where is the line between a diagnosable clinical illness and normal human suffering? When do these normal emotions change into something more sinister?

It's a tricky question to answer, because the line that separates mental health from mental illness lies not between people but down the centre of every human being. It's not like that group of people is mentally ill and this group is perfectly well. We all have within us the potential for mental illness or mental well-being.

BOX 2.1 MY STORY

What makes me an expert in burnout and mental health at work?

First of all, I'm a qualified and registered clinical psychologist and executive coach. That means I have a pretty unique view of mental health at work, from both a clinical and business perspective. I've worked with organisations as diverse as the UK Cabinet Office, Novartis and Sony to develop workplace mental well-being initiatives.

I also had a rather harrowing introduction to mental health at work.

Back in the 1980s, I was working as an ambulanceman in central London. It was 12 December 1988, and I was on the early shift – seven a.m. to three p.m. It was early in the morning, and we'd been out on our first call of the day. My crewmate, Kevin, and I were returning to our station, driving down Millbank, along the banks of the Thames. It was a beautiful sunny winter's day and the river was uncharacteristically blue. We were just approaching Lambeth Bridge when the radio bleeped and announced our call sign.

"Standby, Waterloo One. I have a Call Red Accident for you." The phrase 'Call Red Accident' meant it was an emergency.

"Waterloo One, it's a Call Red Accident to Clapham Junction Station. A train crash. No further information at this time. To you at 08.14, Alpha Tango, Waterloo One."

I read about the details of the call and added my initials to those of the dispatcher. "Alpha Tango, Mike Delta, Waterloo One, on our way."

Off we went, blue lights pulsing and siren wailing, to Clapham Junction. Kevin forced his way through the rush hour traffic, driving in an almost military fashion. My heart was pumping and thoughts were tumbling through my mind. We didn't know what to expect.

As we raced up the Wandsworth Road to Clapham, the radio bleeped again.

"Waterloo One, this is a major incident. I say again, this is a major incident. Two, possibly three, trains have collided. There are multiple casualties with multiple fatalities. I say again, this is a major incident. We'll keep you informed."

We arrived a few minutes later, and saw a police car and ambulance already there, blue lights flashing. *Oh God*, I thought, *we're only the second ambulance on the scene.*

I clambered up the embankment to behold a scene of horror. Two trains had collided and concertinaed upwards. A third train lay on its side beside the arch made by the other two. We later found out that the two trains had collided head-on; then, as the survivors were trying to escape, the wreckage was hit by a third train.

People, red with blood, were wandering around. We could hear screaming and crying, and the hiss of the train wreck. Some of the injured were being comforted by teenagers from the Emanuel School, which overlooked the railway track.

It was chaotic and terrifying. I looked around and saw there were fewer than ten of us – police officers and ambulance crew – with hundreds of injured and dying people.

I spent 14 hours at the scene, first of all looking after the people who had survived, and later helping to remove the deceased.

I have lots of memories of Clapham, and they're just that – memories. But I also see dead people. I have video clips – vivid, animated pictures – of Clapham in my mind, and these are different to the memories. What I see is as clear and real as it was when I first witnessed the event, 30 years ago. The smells, the sounds, the fear – I feel it all.

The dead people who are right there, in my mind, are women. The first is a young woman killed in one of the carriages. She has blonde hair and wide blue eyes that are staring. She is wearing a Burberry mac. Her hands are still holding on tight to a carrier bag filled with gift-wrapped presents – for an office Christmas party, I guess, or an after-work visit to family or friends.

The second woman's eyes are closed. She has dark hair and is wearing jeans and a red Berghaus walking jacket. We were taking her up the embankment on a rescue stretcher when her London Transport travel card fell from her coat pocket. I looked down at the photo of her on the card, smiling and alive, and then at her body on the stretcher, and I started to cry.

I got home at about one o'clock in the morning. I went to make myself a mug of tea, and that's when I first noticed that something was wrong. I tried to drink my tea, but my hands were shaking so much – not trembling, but really shaking – that tea slopped over the rim of the mug.

Over the coming weeks, I would get nightmares. Oddly enough, not about Clapham, but nightmares of being involved in other transport accidents – I'd be a passenger in a car crash, or on an aeroplane as the engines failed and we plummeted to Earth. That's also when I began seeing the dead people. I'd be doing something mundane, like washing up, and I'd look up and find those blue eyes gazing into mine.

(*Continued*)

The day after the Clapham rail crash, I went into work at seven o'clock in the morning. As you might expect, there was an atmosphere of disbelief and shock at the station. Some of my colleagues were numb, dazed; some were wired. I think we all felt a mixture of sadness and confusion, if that's the right word.

Discussing the events of Clapham was frowned upon by the station officer. We were expected to just get on with things. After all, we were paramedics who saw dead, dying and injured people every day; it was part of the job. Of course, that was true – but Clapham was different.

I didn't mention my symptoms. I'm sure if I had, I'd have been sent off to occupational health. But it would also have been the end of my career as a paramedic.

Over time, the symptoms got worse. I know now that I was suffering with symptoms of post-traumatic stress disorder. But I didn't get any help. I just accepted my lot and managed the best I could.

The following September, I left the London Ambulance Service to study for a degree in social psychology at the London School of Economics. After I graduated, I pursued a career in clinical psychology, specialising in psychological trauma (I wonder why that was?). Now, I run a consulting and coaching business, specialising in well-being at work – especially mental well-being at work.

What is the difference between normal human emotion and mental illness?

Feeling lousy is part of the human condition; indeed, it is a part of what makes us human. We all feel sad, upset, angry, fearful and despairing at times. Sometimes, we feel all of these emotions and more in an average day. That's just normal. The question is, when does normal emotion become an illness?

Imagine a scale from 0 (normal) to 10 (clinical disorder). From week to week, from day to day and even from hour to hour our sense of mental well-being moves up and down this scale. We might begin the day feeling great – at 2 on the scale. Then we have a stressful day at work and we move up to 6. The commute home is worse than normal and we are up to 8. After we get through the front door, close the door and get into our pajamas, we are back to 2 once more.

When we were at 8, we were in a state of poor mental health, but a temporary state. Mental health isn't black and white – it fluctuates. The population isn't divided into the mentally healthy and the mentally ill. We all experience 'mental illness' for chunks of our lives – it's a universal experience. The time we spend at the extreme end of the scale can vary between a few minutes or hours, or even months.

What separates normal human emotion from mental illness is how long we spend at the illness end of the scale. With normal emotion, a person's time at the top of the scale is temporary. With mental illness, a person gets stuck at the 10. The person feels hopeless and helpless. They are convinced that they will feel as they do for the rest of their life and there is absolutely nothing they can do to change things. It's a truly awful state of mind to be in.

How do mental health professionals diagnose mental illness?

Diagnosing depression, anxiety or any other mental health disorder isn't as simple as it might seem. Fundamentally, four aspects discriminate an abnormal symptom from normal emotion:

- *It gets in the way of the person doing what they'd like to do.* For example, depression stops someone dating because they feel worthless (a normal reaction might be for a person to feel they are 'punching above their weight', but go on the date anyway).
- *It is severe.* For example, a person has a panic attack at work just before an important presentation (a normal reaction might be to feel nervous).
- *It persists for a long time.* For example, a person feels consistently and pervasively upset for longer than two weeks.
- *The person can't see an end to the emotional state or any sense of being able to control it.* For example, they feel stuck in the feeling, rather than thinking, *I feel terrible now but I know I'll feel better in a few days – I always do.*

Establishing a mental well-being baseline

In this book I am advocating that managers take a far more proactive stance about mental well-being in their workplaces. As a manager, you can do this by promoting mental well-being in your realm of influence. An easy way to begin this is by becoming more attuned to the mental well-being of the people you work with.

Spend a bit of time thinking about your colleagues and their personalities. What is each person like on an average day? How do they respond when they are under stress? How sociable are they? Which are the team members who are punctual and conscientious, and who will more often than not arrive late for meetings? Which members of staff always leave the workplace promptly at the end of the day and who tends to work late and even take work home? Who habitually dresses smartly and who is more casual in their attire?

Most good managers will know all of the above, but the information is usually stored in our minds in a vague and unfocused way. Take some time to reflect on this knowledge and make it as conscious as you can. To be able to spot 'abnormal' changes in people, you need to know what their 'normal' looks like.

I used to sit near someone at the West Bromwich Albion football ground who was fondly known as 'Meldrew' because of his habit of constantly complaining about almost everything. I knew him for years and he didn't change much. I am sure he was just as morose in his home and work life.

Imagine for a moment that you are a new manager who doesn't know what Meldrew is like. You might easily see an emerging depression. But for Meldrew, his *normal* is equivalent to most people's *miserable*.

Some people have a low baseline, like Meldrew. Other people might be the opposite and have a baseline of unrelenting positivity and enthusiasm. However, most people are pretty average in their emotional baseline – not too up or down.

To be able to spot the early warning signs of poor mental health you need to be alert for any significant deviation from the individual's normal baseline functioning.

Spotting the early warning signs: things to look out for

Quality of work

Has the quality of the person's work declined recently?

Time taken to do the work

Is it taking the person longer than expected to complete work tasks? In depression, one of the first symptoms that becomes apparent is difficulty in concentration and memory. People who are becoming anxious will start to worry whether their work is good enough and start repeatedly checking what they do, which slows things down.

Working hours – arriving late or working long hours

Is a person who is usually punctual frequently arriving late? They may be sleeping poorly, which is a symptom of both depression and anxiety. Is somebody working unusually long hours? They may be finding it hard to focus and so have to do extra hours just to keep up with their work.

Workplace relationships

You need to act if the person's distress starts spilling out and affecting other people in the team. Are colleagues of the person approaching you to express concern for their welfare? Conversely, are colleagues complaining because they feel the person isn't pulling their weight?

Is someone in the team being particularly irritable, snappy or belligerent? Conversely, is a normally confident person behaving in a clingy or dependent manner? Do they seem in constant need of support and encouragement? Both irritability and clinginess can be signs of an emerging depression or anxiety disorder.

Appearance and manner (clean and tidy or disheveled)

Does the person turn up at work looking untidy, with poor personal hygiene, or dressed inappropriately? This might be a sign of self-neglect, which often happens with a mood disorder.

Depression at work

The most common mental health difficulties you will encounter at work are depression and anxiety. This section outlines depression; see the later section 'Anxiety at work' for details on anxiety.

What is depression?

In January 1945, John Steinbeck published his brilliant novel *Cannery Row*. In it he describes a marine biologist collecting samples. He writes that some creatures are so delicate it's impossible to 'catch' them. Instead, you have to put your collecting bucket into the ocean and allow these creatures to slowly crawl in.

Describing depression (or any other mental disorder) is a bit like this. Medical labels and psychological jargon are too crude to describe the experience of mental distress. Instead, the description of a complex human experience, like one of Steinbeck's delicate sea creatures, has to emerge by itself before the scalpel of the clinician begins to cut it up.

The actual lived experience of depression is far better captured, in fact, in art, literature and poetry than in medical textbooks.

The Scream

In the dying days of the 19th century, the Norwegian Expressionist painter Edvard Munch created one of the most famous images in modern art: *The Scream* (Munch, 1893). It is a disturbing and evocative depiction of mental illness. Google it now, if you can, and take a look. The painting shows a figure standing on a bridge with a background of dark, swirling oranges and blues. The figure holds its head in its hands and there is an agonised expression – a scream – on its skull-like face. I say 'its' because the figure is androgynous. In the background, two other figures can be seen strolling, seemingly unaware of the anguish of the main figure.

The Scream tells you as much as you need to know about the experience of depression. There is the expression on the face of deep anguish, torment and hopeless. The surrounding world is dark, threatening and unstable. Other people are separate beings living a different life and disconnected to the screaming figure. Finally, the screamer is standing on a bridge, between one state and another, perhaps with a hint of the possibility of suicide.

The picture encapsulates many of the emotions and beliefs common in depression. You can see the desperation. You can sense the darkness of the world and the feeling of isolation from others.

'Not Waving but Drowning'

The British poet Stevie Smith also evoked the hopelessness and helplessness of depression in her 1957 poem 'Not Waving but Drowning' (Smith, 1983). The poem tells of a man who is drowning, but his desperate signals for help are misinterpreted as waving because of his habit of hiding his feelings by larking around.

'Not Waving but Drowning' is a powerful metaphor for the experience of depression. Stevie Smith says it was cold, but had always been too cold for the drowning man. She talks about him being too far out, farther than he thought, and adds that he had always been too far out.

She is talking about both a feeling and a situation. It's a poem about drowning, both physically and emotionally. The poem describes the coldness, social disconnection and helplessness and hopelessness of depression. Drowning is a metaphor for being consumed by an irresistible force, which is how people with depression often describe the experience. Depressed people often know their feelings are absurd, yet nonetheless feel powerless to resist.

Stevie Smith wrote 'Not Waving but Drowning' when suffering a deep depression. Shortly after writing the poem, she attempted to take her own life.

The psychology of depression

Stevie Smith and Edvard Munch capture the experience of depression in art. But how do psychologists understand depression and try to pin it down in a scientific description?

Depression is a mood disorder. 'Mood' is a sustained emotion that colours the way we view life. Being able to recognise depression is important, because as many as 20 per cent of women and 10 per cent of men are clinically depressed and the numbers are rising.

In order to be diagnosed with depression a person must have five of the following nine symptoms:

- **Low mood:** most of nearly every day, the person feels depressed or looks depressed to other people.
- **Lack of interest:** most of nearly every day, the person lacks interest or pleasure in nearly all activities.

- **Disturbance in eating and weight:** the depressed person loses their appetite and there is often a noticeable loss of weight, despite the fact that they are not dieting.
- **Disturbed sleep:** the person complains of insomnia or excessive tiredness most days. Alternatively, some complain of hypersomnia, which means wanting to sleep all the time.
- **Activity disturbance:** the person often appears to have slowed down. This is often interspersed with periods of intense activity.
- **Fatigue:** most days the person just feels tired and lacking in energy.
- **Low self-worth:** people who are depressed feel worthless.
- **Impaired cognitive functioning:** the depressed person finds it very difficult to concentrate and also experiences memory problems.
- **Thoughts of death:** people who are depressed often have intrusive thoughts about death, dying or suicide.

Burnout and depression

There has been a lot of research looking at burnout and depression. There is a big overlap between the two experiences, but they are not the same thing (Ahola et al., 2005). It is possible to be burnt out and not depressed and vice versa. A Finnish study found that only half of those suffering severe burnout met the criteria for depression (Ahola & Hakanen, 2007). The key difference between the two is that burnout is work related but depression can occur in any context. An interesting Dutch study on burnout and depression in teachers found that a perception of being treated unfairly was related to both depression and burnout. But context was everything. A lack of reciprocity at work (from students) led to burnout, while a lack of reciprocity at home (from the person's spouse) resulted in depression (Bakker et al., 2000). I'd suggest that burnout is best seen as a form of depression that emerges in the context of work.

Anxiety at work

It was the feeling all the time like that feeling you have if you're walking and you slip or trip and the ground is rushing up at you, but instead of lasting half a second, the way that does, it lasted for six months. It's a sensation of being afraid all the time but not even knowing what it is that you're afraid of.

(Solomon, 2013)

The above quote, from Andrew Solomon's 2013 TED talk, expresses with great eloquence the experience of severe anxiety. It is probably the most common mental health problem you will encounter at work. Anxiety takes many different forms, from the panic described by Andrew Solomon to persistent and pervasive worry. It includes feelings of guilt and shame.

Anxiety in fiction

In 1925, Stefan Zweig published his novella *Fear* (Zweig, 2015). *Fear* is about anxiety in its many forms. It tells the story of Irene, a young married woman and successful lawyer. The novella begins with Irene leaving her lover's apartment. As she descends the stairs to the street, she is suddenly overwhelmed by a vague fear:

All at once there was a shape like a black spinning top circling before her eyes, her knees froze in dreadful rigidity and she had to catch hold of the banister rail in haste to keep herself from falling abruptly forwards.

(Zweig, 2015)

Irene is then confronted by her lover's former mistress, who blackmails her and threatens to reveal the affair to Irene's kind and decent husband. As the story develops, Irene is paralysed with anxiety, shame and guilt, despite her husband giving her numerous opportunities to confess and be forgiven.

What is anxiety disorder?

Every day we hear people (or ourselves) say how 'stressed' they feel. However, when people talk about stress at work or feeling stressed, they are really talking about feeling anxious.

Stress and anxiety are different. Stress is something in the outside world that happens to you. Anxiety is your reaction to stress. It's an important distinction to make. Stress will always be out there. It's not going to go away, and there is a good chance it will get worse. Stress is hard to control, but how that stress affects us is under our control. That external stress can result in us feeling anxious, excited or not much at all. The important factor isn't the stress but the meaning we attach to it – how we interpret it.

BOX 2.2 WHY IS ANXIETY CAUSED BY PERCEPTION NOT REALITY?

Recently, I took a taxi in central London. The traffic was awful because of a demonstration. However, my journey was very pleasant. My driver was called Vera and she was from Brazil. She told me about her life in London and how much she missed her family back home. Although she was chatting away, she was making good progress through the traffic. I arrived at my office relaxed and cheerful – despite the horrible London traffic.

Later that day, I took another taxi to the station. The driver was, to put it mildly, very agitated. As soon as I got in the car, we were off at speed. Foot down, accelerating fast into the traffic jam and then slamming the brakes on. He spent the whole journey commenting on other drivers, calling them names under his breath. When I arrived at the station, I was beginning to feel quite anxious myself.

These two taxi drivers showed how human beings can respond differently to environmental stress.

Vera accepted that she couldn't do very much about the traffic; she could only do her best to get where she was going, while chatting away and making the best of the situation. She understood that the traffic was bad and that becoming cross and upset about it would not change anything. She was firmly in charge of her own emotional responses to that situation. Vera had the ability to take a step back, observe what was going on and decide how she would respond. In turn, her good-natured response affected me: because she was calm and relaxed, so was I.

On the other hand, the second cab driver just seemed to get caught up in the situation without pausing for a moment to think about what was happening and how best to respond. His emotional responses were being controlled by the external environment. His anxiety influenced his behaviour and driving style, which made him even more anxious. I dread to think how he felt at the end of the day, because I felt worn out at the end of the ten-minute cab ride.

In these two situations, the environment was a constant: both drivers were driving in heavy London traffic. Yet one was calm and the other agitated. The difference wasn't the traffic (the outside presence of stress); it was the meaning each attached to the situation.

The psychology of anxiety

People who experience anxiety constantly worry about the future and the bad things that might happen (whereas depressed people constantly think about the past and how unfair their life has been).

Anxious people see threats everywhere. They approach life with the attitude that if something can go wrong, it will go wrong – and if it does go wrong, the consequences will be catastrophic for them.

This distorted way of perceiving the world can make it tricky to help the anxious person. Let's imagine for a moment you are concerned about a member of staff, Sam, who seems on edge and flustered. You want to help, and so you approach Sam in your best affable manager manner.

"Hi, Sam," you say. "Is everything okay?"

Even though you only have the best intentions, Sam hears, *"I've noticed that you're not coping. I'm not happy and I've got my eye on you, buddy."*

Sam perceived your innocent attempt to help as criticism because that's what anxiety can do to our thinking: it distorts the way we perceive the world and other people. In other words, everything is a threat and must either be escaped from or fought against.

Why stress can be a good thing – good stress and bad stress

In 1908, two psychologists, Robert Yerkes and John Dodson, studied the relationship between stress and performance (Yerkes & Dodson, 1908). As a result of their research, they came up with a model that has become a classic in psychology. It's known as the Yerkes–Dodson curve (see Figure 2.1).

This graph expresses the relationship between how stressed you are and how well you perform at a task. The curve shows that when stress is low, performance is correspondingly low. In other words, if you're bored and there's no challenge or stimulation at work then the quality of your work is likely to be poor. However, as stimulation and stress increase, so does performance. If your job has more of a sense of urgency and importance, you're likely to do it better. So in this sense stress (which everybody seems to think of as being a bad thing) can be very positive – but only up to a

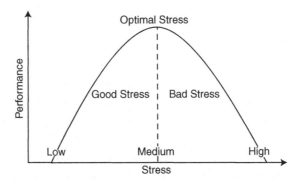

Figure 2.1 The Yerkes–Dodson curve.

point. At the top of the stress curve is a point that produces optimal performance. But what happens if stress continues to increase? We can see from
the Yerkes–Dodson curve that if stress continues to increase, performance
rapidly drops off, eventually becoming very poor. When this happens consistently, it results in burnout.

So, too much stress is very bad for you. But too little stress is also bad for
you. Yerkes and Dodson found that stress can actually be a positive force,
if it's managed properly. This applies both to you as an individual and to
teams and organisations.

Stress in itself isn't good or bad; it's simply another force to be managed. By understanding and managing stress you can learn how to improve performance – both your own and that of the people you lead. When
stress reaches its optimal level and you're flying, you get a real buzz. This
is what the psychologist Mihaly Csikszentmihalyi (pronounced Me-high
Chick-sent-me-high) calls flow (Csikszentmihalyi, 1990). This state of mind
happens when you're fully immersed in an activity, feeling energised and
focused. You're so involved in what you're doing that it's like the rest of the
world doesn't exist. This is good stress, or eustress.

Entitled organisations and fearful organisations

In her 1995 book, *Danger in the Comfort Zone*, the psychologist and management writer Judith Bardwick applied the Yerkes–Dodson model to teams

and organisations (Bardwick, 1995). She described organisations and individuals at the left-hand, low-stress end of the curve as suffering from a sense of entitlement. She argued that businesses at this end of the curve seem more interested in avoiding risk than adding value. In such *entitled organisations*, the staff feel that their jobs are safe and that to earn a salary they simply have to turn up and look busy. Employees are more interested in maintaining a quiet life than doing a good job. They are rarely held to account for the quality of their work performance, and so they often don't perform particularly well. Instead, they become complacent ("Anything for a quiet life") or apathetic ("No one cares what I do here anyway, so why bother?"). This type of organisation is usually more prevalent in the public sector than in the private sector. However, it's also noticeable in banking, where in some sectors people are paid massive bonuses irrespective of results.

At the other end of the spectrum to entitled organisations are those that are exposed to too much stress – these are the *fearful organisations*. People work long hours for little appreciation. They over-work because they're terrified of losing their jobs. This has an emotional impact on the workforce. People become anxious, resentful and cynical. Morale slumps and along with it, performance and productivity.

The best companies to work for are those that lie in the centre of the curve – organisations where there is a sense of energy and enthusiasm and buzz, where there are opportunities to achieve and where employees have a sense of control over their work and feel appreciated and valued for what they do. This medium level of pressure pushes performance, productivity and general well-being massively upwards.

Burnout and mental health problems emerge in the context of an organisational culture. At an individual level, burnout emerges in the context of an individual employee's personality. That is what I will explore in the next chapter.

Chapter takeaways

- There is a strong relationship between burnout and mental ill health.
- Burnout is mental ill health that occurs in the context of work.

- It's normal to feel depressed or anxious from time to time – negative emotion is part of the human condition.
- Feeling depressed or anxious turns into burnout or a clinical depression or anxiety disorder when:
  - The feelings stop you participating in your normal day-to-day life.
  - You are convinced that you will feel depressed or anxious for the rest of your life and you feel helpless to do anything about it.
- The right amount of stress is good for you. Too much or too little is harmful.

References

Ahola, K. & Hakanen, J. (2007). 'Job Strain, Burnout, and Depressive Symptoms: A Prospective Study among Dentists'. *Journal of Affective Disorders, 104*(1–3), 103–10. Retrieved from https://doi.org/10.1016/j.jad.2007.03.004.

Ahola, K., Honkonen, T., Isometsä, E., Kalimo, R., Nykyri, E., Aromaa, A. & Lönnqvist, J. (2005). 'The Relationship Between Job-related Burnout and Depressive Disorders – Results from the Finnish Health 2000 Study'. *Journal of Affective Disorders, 88*(1), 55–62. Retrieved from https://doi.org/10.1016/j.jad.2005.06.004.

Bakker, A., Schaufeli, W. B., Demerouti, E., Janssen, P. P. M., Van Der Hulst, R. & Brouwer, J. (2000). 'Using Equity Theory to Examine the Difference Between Burnout and Depression'. *Anxiety, Stress and Coping, 13,* 247–69.

Bardwick, J. M. (1995). *Danger in the Comfort Zone.* New York: American Management Association.

Csikszentmihalyi, M. (1990). *Flow.* New York: Harper and Row.

Munch, E. (1893). *The Scream. Oil, Pastel and Casein on Cardboard. 91 x 73.5 cm.* Oslo: National Gallery.

Smith, S. (1983). *Collected Poems.* New York: New Directions Publishing.

Solomon, A. (2013). 'Depression, the Secret We Share'. *Talk Video | TED.Com,* pp. 1–10. Retrieved from http://www.ted.com/talks/andrew_solomon_depression_the_secret_we_share.

Yerkes, R. M. & Dodson, J. D. (1908). 'The Relation of Strength of Stimulus to Rapidity of Habit-Formation'. *Journal of Comparative Neurology and Psychology, 18,* 459–82.

Zweig, S. (2015). *Fear.* London: Pushkin Press.

3

BURNOUT AND PERSONALITY

Burnout happens because of the pressures of work. So why doesn't everyone in a workplace burn out? The experience of burnout involves exhaustion, cynicism and declining performance and productivity. Burnout is also influenced by context: the workplace context determines whether a person will become burnt out. What actually triggers the individual to burn out and the way that the burnout is expressed will be determined by the context of the individual's personality. We are all different, and whether burnout emerges due to a given work situation is influenced by the type of person we are. Our different personalities explain why some people are more resilient than others and why you might quite like a particular environment while someone else might hate the same environment. This chapter will unpack the concept of personality and explain what psychologists mean by the term. We all have five different factors that interact to form the whole we call our personality. I will discuss these five factors and how they are related to burnout. I will also explore the types of personality that are particularly vulnerable to burnout.

Let's begin with a real world example that illustrates how personality is the mediating factor between environmental stress and burnout.

BOX 3.1 JOHN AND JAMES

John is a natural worrier. For as long as he can remember he has been an anxious person. Like many anxious people, John is very conscientious and works hard. He is also bright, and because of his hard work and intelligence he does well at the computer games company where he works. One day his boss asks him if he'd like to take on a new challenge and head up the department where he has worked for the past eight years. At first John feels pleased and proud to be promoted to head of department. However, his pleasure soon turns to anguish when he realises that managing a team under pressure isn't as easy as he thought. Then, he is made responsible for an important project which requires a great deal of planning and meetings with internal and external stakeholders. He begins to worry that he isn't up to the task. He can't sleep and partly because of this he finds it increasingly difficult to focus and his performance deteriorates.

James works for the same organisation. He is very different to John, being a lively extrovert with lots of ideas. He also gets promoted to a head of department role. Like John, he enjoys it at first; but he soon comes to realise that in his new senior role he has to really toe the corporate line. His manager, the CEO, is a controlling person, and James feels micro-managed and resentful that he can't speak his mind as much as he would like. Things come to a head when James's manager takes him to one side and criticises him for wearing brown shoes at the office. James feels demotivated, cynical and depressed. He lies awake at night thinking of what he'd like to tell his boss, which leaves him feeling increasingly resentful and angry.

James and John have very different personalities. James is outgoing and open to new ideas. He gets bored easily and relishes change. In contrast, John is very introverted and socially conservative. He hates change. Both have taken the first steps on the road to burnout. Ironically, if we swapped them around so that James was given John's job and vice versa, they would probably both be fine. John would enjoy the stability of knowing exactly what was expected of him and James would enjoy the prospect of change, meeting new people and the challenges that really worry John.

In 2006, France Télécom was in financial difficulties and its CEO, Didier Lombard, pursued a policy to 'encourage' staff members to accept voluntary redundancy. Lombard told managers that unwanted staff would "leave by the window or the door". This strategy was implemented by giving staff unattainable performance objectives, moving employees to new jobs in far away locations and redeploying employees into jobs that didn't remotely suit their personalities. The company moved shy, introverted people to sales where they would be instructed to persistently cold call prospective customers. Employees who were very extraverted, gregarious and affable (in fact, the sort of people who might like cold calling) would be isolated and given monotonous data entry jobs. It was a strategy that worked and many people gladly took redundancy. Unfortunately, it also resulted in dozens of the more emotionally fragile employees taking their own lives.

In a sensational and landmark court case in 2019, the company, since rebranded Orange, was convicted of "institutional moral harassment", and the 77-year-old Lombard was given a 12-month prison sentence. His deputy, and the human resources director, received the same sentence. The judges upheld the full prosecution argument that France Télécom had consciously implemented a plan to humiliate staff into leaving the company as a way of dodging France's strong job protection laws (Chrisafis, 2019; Bremner, 2019).

I could speculate on the personality characteristics of M. Lombard, but I won't because this isn't relevant to our discussion. However, he and his senior management colleagues did demonstrate a low cunning by understanding and using the personality traits of their employees as an instrument to cause suffering.

Let's go beyond this low cunning understanding and unpack what psychologists mean when they write about personality.

What is personality?

That sounds like an easy question, but it isn't. We sort of understand that everybody is different, but we tend to understand that at a superficial level. The reason is that we see the world through the lens of our own personality. We think that the way we perceive the world is rational, accurate and objective. *I know that I am a reasonable, rational and averagely intelligent person and so my understanding of the world must be pretty accurate; I see the world as it is.* The big problem with that statement is, it just isn't true. If it were true, everybody would see the world in more or less the same way. There would be no disagreement about whom to vote for, Brexit or which football team to support. I mean, how is it that two intelligent, well-educated and generally decent people can tear each other apart and express real hatred for each other when discussing something like Brexit? Of course, there are lots of reasons, but one of the factors is that we don't experience reality as it is, but instead experience a perception of reality that is distorted by the lens of our personality.

A good way to understand personality is to think of it as being a bit like the psychological equivalent of our immune system. Our immune system protects us from all the nasty bacteria, viruses and infectious agents in our environment. If we have a strong immune system, it is easily able to fight off these pathogens. However, if our immune system is weakened, these infectious agents can invade the body, take hold and make us ill. Our immune system exists to protect our physical health.

In the same way, our personality serves to protect our mental and emotional health. We all live in a world full of stress, challenges and pressure. It is our personality, which includes coping skills and the ability to adapt, that determines whether we respond constructively to these challenges or succumb to them. When we succumb to the challenges in the work environment, we call this burnout.

The big five model of personality

If we accept the idea of personality as a kind of psychological immune system then the next question to ask is: how do we explain why people are different? Why does one specific stressful event, let's say having to give a presentation to an audience of 500 colleagues, send John off the scale with anxiety, while James would relish the same event?

Like many words, personality has a common, day-to-day meaning ("she has a great personality!") as well as a technical meaning.

When psychologists talk about personality they are generally referring to our individual and enduring differences in thinking, feeling and behaving. Over the years, psychologists have come up with different models to explain personality. The most widely accepted model currently is the big five model, or more correctly, the five-factor model of personality (McCrae & Costa, 2006; Soto et al., 2015).

According to the big five model, our personality is made up of five factors, which are enduring patterns of thought, feeling and behaviour that remain stable across our life span. The five factors are:

- Extraversion,
- Neuroticism,
- Openness to experience,
- Agreeableness,
- Conscientiousness.

We all have greater or lesser 'amounts' of these factors. This isn't quite how it's done, but imaging giving yourself a score from 0–10 on each of the factors, and the resulting scores would provide a crude 'map' of your personality. Our scores are on a continuum, so we can be high or low or somewhere in between. There are many online tests you can do that will give you an approximation of your big five personality structure.

No value judgement is attached to being high or low on any of the factors. Being high or low on, say, openness, brings both advantages and disadvantages.

The five factors can be remembered easily using the acronym OCEAN. I'll describe them in the following sections.

(O) Openness

Openness describes how open to new ideas and experiences a person is. People high on openness are intellectually curious, they enjoy new experiences and they actually like change (remember James in the earlier example). In a work setting, being high on openness is valuable as long as it is combined with high conscientiousness. This is because the conscientiousness ensures that the creative ideas generated by high openness get channelled into concrete activity and outcomes. If a person is high on openness but low on conscientiousness, they have the ability to generate creative ideas but then get easily distracted, and so nothing comes of their creative ideas.

It's easy to see that a person who is high on openness would be vulnerable to burnout in a very ordered, constrained and rule-driven organisation. Some highly rule-driven organisations have developed sections that accommodate and make the best of their high-openness employees. For example, the police force has detectives and undercover officers, and the army has Special Forces regiments.

(C) Conscientiousness

Conscientiousness describes a person's tendency to work hard and be reliable. A person high on conscientiousness has the attitudes and behaviours that are compatible with achieving goals. It is the personality factor that best predicts the difference between *potential* to achieve and *actual* achievement. There are two main parts (or facets) to conscientiousness: industriousness and orderliness. Industrious people work hard and orderly people like their life to be ordered – 'everything in its place and a place for everything'.

High conscientiousness is generally a positive characteristic to possess. However, like all personality factors, it has a downside. When highly conscientious people are placed under a lot of external stress, they can easily turn into anxious, micro-managing workaholics.

People low on conscientiousness, meanwhile, are life's laidback 'surfer dude' characters. These folk plod on not achieving much, and they're pretty much impervious to stress and anxiety. However, when stress gets too much for them, their behaviour can easily descend into complete chaos where even the basics don't get done.

(E) Extraversion

People who are high on extraversion are really interested in other people and get a lot of their energy from being around others and interacting with them. Think of it like this: if a person is interested in stamps, they pay attention to them; if not, they are bored by them. Similarly, if someone is interested in people, they pay them a lot of attention and are fascinated by them. On the other hand, people who are low on extraversion, aren't that interested in other people and don't need others around them to maintain their energy. They are reflective people who enjoy their own company and their own thoughts. To use the above example, they are happy with their stamp collection (or whatever their interest is), thinking about things and daydreaming.

Like conscientiousness, extraversion is one of the personality factors that predicts success in most types of work. Extraverted people, as you might imagine, are good at building positive relationships.

The two main parts to extraversion are enthusiasm and assertiveness. Extraverted people bring a high level of energy to what they do and are assertive – in other words, they find it easy to express their opinions. Again, it sounds like it's a positive thing to be extraverted. It can be, but in the wrong work environment it can be a disaster. If the extraverted person isn't kept busy (think of James), they can be a bit like a boisterous puppy, always demanding a lot of attention. They become the annoying person who wanders around the office wanting to chat to everyone and distracting others from getting on with their work.

The person low on extraversion is best described as being shy, and they will quietly get on with things without having to be constantly reassured or chased. However, if a person like this, is suddenly put into a role where they have to interact a lot with other people, then their anxiety levels will rise. They will start to feel somewhat uncomfortable. If you are a person who is low on extraversion, you will eventually find that being around too many people, too often, will be exhausting.

This situation sometimes happens when a person who is low on extraversion is promoted to management or a supervisory role. The reason for the promotion is that they were very good at their job, which may have been quite a solitary job. In other words, they were technically excellent. Because of this, they are offered promotion to a supervisory role – maybe a team leader. This new role involves lots of contact with other people. They have to attend and speak at meetings. They might be asked to set career development goals for people in their team and performance manage other people. If you are not particularly extrovert, all these tasks can feel very stressful and exhausting. This is the situation that faced John in the example above. People lacking in extraversion often make poor line managers because they either retreat to their previous 'technical' job, or conversely try their best to make a go at being a good line manager, but quickly find that they become so tired and stressed, they just can't do it, and end up leaving or going off sick. The France Télécom example above, is a good example of what can happen if the person is assigned a role that conflicts with their basic personality make up. It can be disastrous.

It's easy to see how both high and low levels of extraversion can result in vulnerability to burnout in a stressful work environment. However, like everything in life, nothing is black and white. For example, consider a highly extraverted bank clerk who enjoys chatting to customers. If he is told that the queues at his counter are getting too long at the bank and he has to stop the chitchat with customers and hurry things up, he will be unhappy. One of his main motivators, flowing from his personality, has just been removed and his journey to burnout has begun. This also works the other way, with a shy bank clerk who is asked to be a bit friendlier with the customers.

(A) Agreeableness

In everyday language, agreeableness is synonymous with being friendly and likeable. While people high on agreeableness do tend to be friendly and likeable, in personality theory the term is used more literally to mean the tendency to want to agree with other people. People high on agreeableness are very good at rubbing along with others and creating high levels of coherence in teams. Those low on agreeableness can be antagonistic and a bit cantankerous. Agreeableness is made up of two parts: politeness (perhaps a better word is respectfulness) and compassion.

People high on agreeableness are great to work with and increase the positive energy in a workplace. However, they are also highly prone to being influenced by other people and can seem wishy-washy in their opinions. On the other hand, people low on agreeableness will stand their ground in a dispute and are seen as straightforward characters who speak their mind.

Those who are high on agreeableness become very anxious in a highly stressful or conflict-ridden workplace. Also, because they are compassionate people, they have a tendency to prioritise other people's needs above their own. This can lead to their taking on tasks that they don't have the time or skills to finish, because they struggle to say no. The result may be overwork, feelings of resentment and sometimes passive-aggressive resistance. Conversely, if a person low on agreeableness has to work in an organisation that does not tolerate conflict then they will become very anxious, resentful and angry. There are two main types of organisation that can't tolerate conflict: one that is beset with chronic niceness, with the conflict just bubbling away beneath the surface, and one that has a highly buttoned-up, controlled environment where even the mildest dissent is stamped on.

(N) Neuroticism

Neuroticism, or emotional adjustment as it is sometimes called, predicts how well a person copes with life's ups and downs. It is the personality factor most associated with risk of burnout. People high on neuroticism are prone to experiencing high levels of negative emotion, particularly anxiety and despondency. These are associated with thoughts of being under threat. There are two parts to neuroticism: withdrawal and volatility. People high on neuroticism live much of their life in flight-or-fight mode. They cope with high levels of stress in the environment by either withdrawing and avoiding the situation or becoming volatile – touchy, angry and hostile. They are life's worriers. It's easy to see why such people are very vulnerable to burnout.

How can people who are high on neuroticism contribute much value to an organisation? Well, they can add a lot of value, because they have an almost supernatural ability to sniff out potential trouble before anyone else even sees it coming. If more people with higher than average neuroticism had been working for Lehman Brothers, Barings and RBS, the 2008 banking crisis probably wouldn't have happened. People high on neuroticism make excellent lawyers, compliance officers and health and safety officers. The world needs people who are sensitive to threats. Sometimes, it's right to be worried.

People who are low on the personality trait of neuroticism, are probably the group who are at least prone to suffering burnout. They tend to be emotionally stable, grounded and even tempered. They tend to take high levels of stress in their stride, and find it relatively easy to switch off at the end of the day. Generally speaking, being a person who is lower in neuroticism is a positive attribute. The only downside to it is that such people can sometimes be too overly optimistic, trusting and may be Pollyanna-ish. Charles Dickens character Mr Micawber from *David Copperfield* is a good example of a person who is low on neuroticism.

Type A personality and burnout

Having a Type A personality makes it much more likely that you will experience burnout, along with a lot of other unpleasant things, particularly heart disease (Rosenman et al., 1975). These are classic aspects of the Type A personality:

- Highly competitive.
- Very self-critical.
- Easily wound up, with a tendency to overreact.
- Impatient, with a constant sense of time urgency.
- Always multi-tasking, such as checking a mobile phone while eating or watching television.
- Very prone to anger and hostility.
- Tends to see the worse in others.
- Displays a lack of compassion, and sometimes envy and sarcasm.
- Easily falls into bullying behaviour or being the victim of bullies.

Having a Type A personality exists on a continuum, with Type B at the opposing end. Type B people are, as you might expect, the polar opposite of Type A people. Type B people tend to be laidback and relaxed about life, and they tend to be more creative. People with a Type B personality can be just as ambitious and conscientious as those with a Type A personality, but without the high levels of anxiety, volatility and irritability.

In the big five model, people with Type A personalities are those who are high on conscientiousness and neuroticism (particularly the sub-trait of volatility) and low on agreeableness, lacking compassion for others and themselves.

Studies into Type A personality and well-being

Interestingly, Type A personality (and its manifestation, Type A behaviour) wasn't discovered by a psychologist, but by two cardiologists, Meyer Friedman and Ray Rosenman, back in the mid-1950s.

The chairs in the waiting room of their cardiac clinic needed to be frequently repaired and re-upholstered due to wear and tear. The story goes that when the upholsterer arrived to do the work, he pointed out to the cardiologists that the chairs had worn in an unusual way. Most hospital outpatients sit down and wait patiently, but the cardiac patients seemed unable to sit still in their chairs, constantly getting up to ask when they would be seen, and when they did sit, they sat on the edge of the chair and fidgeted. The two cardiologists became curious about this observation and this curiosity triggered years of research that led to the identification of Type A personality as being a bigger predictor of cardiac disease than smoking. Friedman and Rosenman found that more than twice as many Type A people as Type B people developed coronary heart disease. Even when the data was controlled for smoking, age and lifestyle, it still emerged that Type A people were nearly twice as likely to develop heart disease as Type B people. Almost as an afterthought, the two cardiologists commented that a Type A personality made their patients more prone to stress-related illnesses.

That's cardiac disease, but what about Type A personality, burnout and more general psychological well-being? A study looking at nurses in a Canadian hospital (Jamal, 1990) examined the effects of job stress and Type A behaviour on both employee and organisational well-being. The research found that Type A personality employees experienced significantly more job stress and psychosomatic health problems as compared to Type B employees. This is consistent with an earlier study on blue-collar workers (Evans et al., 1987). More recent research in Queensland, Australia, found that the big five model and Type A personality variables were strong predictors of psychological well-being (Hicks & Mehta, 2018). These studies and other research indicate that having a Type A personality is a big predictor of both burnout and poor mental health.

Chapter takeaways

- Whether a person suffers burnout is partly dependent on their personality.
- Differences in personality explain why one person finds a task enjoyable, while a second person finds the same task unbearable.
- The personality is like a psychological immune system.
- Our personality is made up of five factors: openness (our creativity), conscientiousness (our tendency to work hard), extraversion (whether we like being with others), agreeableness (how much we are influenced by others) and neuroticism (how emotionally stable we are).
- Having a Type A personality (competitive, impatient and aggressive) is a big risk factor for burnout.

References

Bremner, C. (2019). 'Ex-France Télécom Bosses Convicted of Bullying Staff into Suicides'. *The Times*, 21 December. Retrieved from https://www.thetimes.co.uk/article/former-france-t-l-com-bosses-convicted-of-bullying-over-spate-of-suicides-qq6gg3j7t.

Chrisafis, A. (2019). 'Former France Télécom Bosses Given Jail Terms Over Workplace Bullying'. *Guardian*, 20 December. Retrieved from https://www.theguardian.com/world/2019/dec/20/former-france-telecom-bosses-jailed-over-workplace-bullying.

Evans, G. W., Palsane, M. N. & Carrere, S. (1987). 'Type A Behavior and Occupational Stress: A Cross-cultural Study of Blue-collar Workers'. *Journal of Personality and Social Psychology, 52*(5), 1002–7. Retrieved from https://doi.org/10.1037/0022-3514.52.5.1002.

Hicks, R. & Mehta, Y. (2018). 'The Big Five, Type A Personality, and Psychological Well-Being'. *International Journal of Psychological Studies, 10*(1), 49. Retrieved from https://doi.org/10.5539/ijps.v10n1p49.

Jamal, M. (1990). 'Relationship of Job Stress and Type-A Behavior to Employees' Job Satisfaction, Organizational Commitment, Psychosomatic Health Problems, and Turnover Motivation'. *Human Relations, 43*(8), 727–38. Retrieved from https://doi.org/10.1177/001872679004300802.

McCrae, R. R. & Costa, P. T. (2006). *Personality in Adulthood: A Five-factor Theory Perspective* (2nd ed.). New York: Guilford Press.

Rosenman, R. H., Brand, R. J., Jenkins, C. D., Friedman, M., Strauss, R., & Wurm, M. (1975). 'Coronary Heart Disease in the Western Collaborative Group Study: Final Follow-up Experience of 8 1/2 Years'. *JAMA MedAss, 233*(8), 872–7.

Soto, C. J., Kronauer, A. & Liang, J. K. (2015). 'Five-Factor Model of Personality'. In *The Encyclopedia of Adulthood and Aging*, pp. 1–5. Retrieved from https://doi.org/10.1002/9781118521373.wbeaa014.

4

OVERCOMING OBSTACLES TO TACKLING BURNOUT

We like to think that anyone with a bit of sensitivity and common sense can see when someone isn't coping, but in fact there are obstacles that get in the way of us being able to help – and often these obstacles are people themselves. Individuals who suffer burnout are often highly conscientious and adept at hiding their distress and putting on a brave face. Managers may well be too busy and preoccupied to spot the signs of that distress. And beneath the surface there are unconscious cognitive biases and coping mechanisms that can make us blind to the suffering of others.

This chapter explores how people can become an obstacle, and offers guidance for how to help those at risk of burnout or suffering burnout – whether your staff or yourself.

Beyond the level of the individual, there are also many obstacles to tackling burnout built into the organisational culture. Section 3 of this book will look at the organisational and systemic obstacles.

What are the obstacles?

Obstacles are things that blocks one's way or prevent or hinders progress.

Why it's important to recognise the obstacles

Any process of culture change – or to be specific, any behaviour change – is not just dependent on knowledge acquisition. While it is important to really understand burnout, just having the knowledge probably won't result in change. You also need to understand what stands in the way of change: the obstacles.

Consider this: We all know and accept that smoking kills, yet many continue to smoke. You can pile on the facts until you are blue in the face and people will continue to smoke. Most people accept that to lose weight we need to eat less and exercise more. Yet if you have ever been on a diet, you've realised that this is easier said than done.

This kind of paradox was addressed back in the 1940s by the German-American psychologist Kurt Lewin in his *force field theory* (Lewin, 1951). Force field theory describes how situations are maintained by a balance between forces that drive change and others that resist change. Lewin said that for change to happen the driving forces must be strengthened and the resisting forces weakened.

Most often people focus on the forces that encourage change and ignore the forces that oppose change. For example, lots of evidence shows that quitting smoking and losing weight are desirable behaviours: they bring health benefits, they make you more attractive and they save you money, to name but a few. However, no matter how many arguments you present to someone and how logically convincing these arguments are, the smoker or overweight person still resists changing their behaviour. This is known as the *fat smoker paradox* (Maister, 2008): in other words, people know what to do, but they just don't do it.

Lewin suggested a different approach. Instead of maximising the arguments for change, he said that those wanting to encourage behaviour change should seek to minimise the reasons not to change – the reasons that oppose change. So for example, smoking cessation campaigns should address people's fears about cravings (nicotine patches), loss of social interaction with other smokers and coping with anxiety.

Obstacle 1: bystander effect

One unconscious cognitive bias that gets in the way of managers' desire to help struggling employees is called *bystander effect* or *diffusion of responsibility*. This is where you observe human suffering but choose not to do anything about it, because you're sure somebody else will act soon.

For example, you might see a perfectly respectably dressed person collapsed in the street. You give them a quick glance but carry on walking. As you do this, your mind is filled with all kinds of thoughts justifying your decision not to do anything. These thoughts might include "Somebody else has probably called an ambulance or something", or "They're probably just drunk" or "Even if I did stop, what could I do?". The problem is, most people walking past the collapsed person will be thinking much the same. Why do people do this? They do it for good reasons: stopping and helping a collapsed person is very anxiety provoking and it represents a threat. Our minds are set up to protect us from threat and from experiencing anxiety, so they quickly generate numerous reasons not to get involved.

Obstacle 2: confirmation bias

Another unconscious process that can get in the way of recognising burnout in others is *confirmation bias* (Kahneman, 2011). This is where we make

---

BOX 4.1 BYSTANDER EFFECT IN ACTION: THE TRAGIC STORY OF KITTY GENOVESE

In March 1964, 28-year-old Kitty Genovese was brutally stabbed to death outside her apartment building in Queens, New York. When the police investigated, they discovered that 38 people had witnessed the various stages of Kitty's murder. When the detectives asked the witnesses why they didn't call the police, most of them replied with a variation of the phrase, "I thought somebody else must have." This dreadful crime and the response of the witnesses was the inspiration for years of research in social psychology into how normal, well-adjusted and intelligent people are able to turn a blind eye to others in distress. Eventually, this phenomena became known as the bystander effect or the diffusion of responsibility (Sanderson, 2020).

up our minds about something and then actively seek evidence to reinforce our belief and actively reject any evidence that disconfirms that belief. This is a very powerful unconscious bias that operates at the most basic perceptual level.

On the Internet you can watch a video in which a group of basketball players are passing a ball around and you are asked to count how many times the players in the white shirts pass the ball (http://www.theinvisiblegorilla.com/videos.html). While you are watching, a person dressed in a gorilla suit walks very obviously across the baseball court, pauses to beat his chest with his arms and casually walks off. When you first see the video, you are likely not to notice the man in the gorilla suit because you are too busy counting the number of times the ball is passed. If you don't notice this, you are in good company, because when shown the video 80 per cent of people don't 'see' the man in the gorilla outfit (Chabris & Simons, 2010). When you're asked to watch the video for the second time, this time looking out for the man in the gorilla suit, his presence becomes blindingly obvious. You fail to see the gorilla first time around simply because you aren't looking for it.

The same thing happens when it comes to noticing that someone is suffering with burnout. Often, you don't see it until it's too late, because you aren't looking for it. If you have developed a belief that Sarah is a competent and resilient person, you tend not to see the signs that she isn't coping, simply because you are not looking for them. You notice all the evidence that suggests that Sarah is doing very well, but your mind unconsciously filters out any evidence that she is in fact struggling. Fast-forward into the future, when Sarah has gone off sick with stress, and you can reflect back on her behaviour and see many clues to her distress. This is common following any bad event. People look back, in hindsight, and say things like, "Oh yes, now you come to mention it, she was looking very tired and stressed." However, because of our unconscious bias we simply do not see this at the time.

Obstacle 3: the overwhelmed manager

Most managers these days are constantly busy, feel overwhelmed themselves much of the time, and are often too preoccupied with the task at hand to even notice the existence of others, let alone subtle early warning signs of burnout. It's often the case that managers aren't uncaring or mean, but just very busy – too busy to offer the support that employees may need. "I'm running an engineering operation here, not a bloody mental hospital," a less-than-sympathetic manager once told me. I disagreed with him for lots of reasons, but I could see his point.

If managers *do* spot the signs of burnout, they often don't feel skilled at helping an employee who appears anxious or withdrawn. Managers have often said to me, "To be honest, I worry about making things worse by saying the wrong thing." Another worry is appearing nosy or intrusive.

All of these factors conspire to induce a manager to turn a blind eye to a person struggling with burnout.

How can I overcome the obstacles?

Step 1: understand the resistance to helping

The first step is to understand that the obstacles exist and are influencing the choices you make. If you are aware of the case of Kitty Genovese and you witness something bad happening, you are far more likely to take the initiative and act, rather than assume someone else will. Similarly, if you are aware that your default position is likely to be 'Do nothing and get on with something else', then if you feel concerned about a colleague at work, you are more likely to pause and consider how you might help.

Step 2: recognise the early warning signs

I describe how you can do this in Chapter 2. Essentially, what you are looking for is any significant change in behaviour. If you are worried about someone, think about what it is that has resulted in your concern. Chances are, the person you are worried about is behaving differently, looks different or is flagging up in some way or another that they are not coping. Often the clues are fairly subtle at first glance, and you might find it difficult to put your finger on why you are concerned. From what you've read in this chapter, you know that this is the tipping point: you can either dismiss your concerns and get on with your work, or pause for a second and reflect on your concerns, why you have them and what you might do that would be helpful to the person.

If ever you have a nagging doubt or concern about someone, you need to stop and reflect on the origins of that semiconscious thought or feeling. Most people tend not to do this, but now that you have read about Kitty Genovese and understand the bystander effect, you no longer have that excuse. You are able to make an informed choice about how to behave.

How to speak to someone suffering from burnout – in small steps

Once you have recognised some of the early warning signs of burnout, it's important to do something and not just turn a blind eye. But how should you approach the person?

Start with yourself

Before you even think about saying something to the person you're worried about, the first step is to manage your own anxiety. Talking to someone who you think might be suffering from burnout is, for most of us, a very anxiety-provoking task. You will find your mind bombarded with all kinds of negative thoughts like, "What if I say the wrong thing and make the situation worse?"

If you recognise that you are feeling anxious or worried about speaking to the person, then you need to prepare mentally for the conversation. Take a deep breath and let your anxiety dissipate along with the negative thoughts. Just acknowledge that what you are going to say might be difficult, but that it's important and it's better to say something than nothing.

In my long career as a clinical psychologist, I have learnt that if you express your concerns to somebody who is suffering in a thoughtful, compassionate, sensible manner then you won't make things worse. Only by being unbelievably crass in what you say or actively malicious would you exacerbate the problem. If you approach someone using your normal level of compassion and common sense then things will be fine.

Pick a suitable spot

Where is it best to have this conversation? In a private meeting room or an open-plan office? In a more informal environment such as the staff restaurant? Some people will like the privacy of a meeting room, while others would find it threatening – like they're being disciplined or interviewed. In this case, they might feel more relaxed talking to you over a cup of coffee in a quiet corner of the staff restaurant or in a coffee shop. Or you could suggest going for a walk together: this avoids too much eye contact, and actually moving along physically can move the conversation along emotionally as well. If you think about the individual and their personality, it will probably be obvious where they might prefer to talk.

Look beneath the mask

So, what do you say if you're worried about someone? That's an easy question to answer: you just ask them how they are. However, don't be surprised if, despite your observations that the person is very distressed, they respond with, "I'm fine, thanks!" People who are suffering often put on a mask of normality. There is still a lot of stigma attached to poor mental health. People often feel embarrassed or ashamed that they not able to cope. They worry that they will be seen as weak, and that this might jeopardise any chances of promotion or even put their job at risk. Therefore, the answer to your question "Are you okay?" is usually "Yes, I am".

The father of psychology, Sigmund Freud identified a number of defence mechanisms that protect us from being overwhelmed by anxiety. His daughter Anna Freud developed these ideas in her important book, *The Ego and the Mechanisms of Defense* (Freud, 1937). These mechanisms of include:

- Denial: where we deny, both to ourselves and other people, that anything is wrong.
- Projection: where we see the anxiety as being located in other people rather than ourselves.
- Rationalisation: where we generate lots of rational reasons to avoid confronting the source of the anxiety.

These Freudian defence mechanisms can be seen in the psychological 'masks' that people put on to avoid talking about their distress (Baim et al., 2002) (or burnout). Here are a few masks that you will encounter if you ask about people's mental health:

- **Mr/Ms Sunshine:** when you ask Mr/Ms Sunshine how they are, you'll get a big smile and they'll say something like, "I'm fine! In fact, I'm really good", and they will go on to give you lots of examples of how life is great. The Mr/Ms Sunshine mask is a noticeable exaggeration of the normal "I'm fine, thanks" response you get when you ask anybody how they are. What differentiates this mask from a normal response is its over-the-top, almost manic quality. This mask is a manifestation of the defence mechanism of denial.
- **Mr/Ms Bullshit:** when you ask Mr/Ms Bullshit how they are, you will get a long, rambling story that never really answers the question. *"Well, yes, I know things are difficult right now, but when I feel like this I remember what one of my old friends used to say to me (what was his name? Frank? No, Nigel? Oh never mind...). He'd say that life is a bit like an onion and there are lots of layers..."* And they go on and on until you either get drawn into their story or get bored and wander off, leaving them alone. This mask is a manifestation of the defence mechanism of intellectualisation.
- **Mr/Ms Caring:** when you ask Mr/Ms Caring how they are, the response will be something along the lines of, "I'm okay, thanks – but how about you? To be honest, I've noticed that you've been looking a bit stressed lately. Are you okay? Is there anything I can do to help?" In other words, they very quickly turn the tables on you, suggesting it's not them who's the stressed one, but you! All the focus then gets shifted from them to you. It's a manifestation of the defence mechanism of projection.
- **Mr/Ms Brick-Wall:** when you ask Mr/Ms Brick-Wall how they are, you'll receive a response of folded arms, no eye contact and a muffled "Fine". Their body language and demeanour will be cut off and saying in no uncertain terms, *Go away and leave me alone.* However, underneath the still and silent demeanour, you can feel the simmering emotion, and that emotion is often rage. This mask is frequently seen in close personal relationships. It's a manifestation of the defence mechanism

of projective identification, where the person experiencing the emotion doesn't verbally tell the other person how they are feeling, but acts in such a way that the other person cannot help but feel it themselves.

- **Mr/Ms Fist:** if the preceding 'masks' or defence mechanisms don't work and you don't go away, you might see Mr/Ms Fist. (Don't panic! I'll tell you how to manage this in the next section.) This is when the person becomes overly aggressive and angry with you. They might say something like, "Look! I'm fine. Just leave me alone – get off my back, won't you!" In terms of defence mechanisms, Mr/Ms Fist is one of the big guns. In fact, it's probably wrong to say that it is a defence mechanism, because what you are seeing is the raw emotion breaking through. Generally speaking, it's not a good thing either for the person or for yourself if they are forced into using this mask.

How to talk to people who reject help

What should you do if your offer of support or help is politely (or even not so politely) rejected?

First of all, if the person seems hostile then back off and give them some space. But don't forget about them. Make sure you go back a bit later when they have had time to calm down and their 'threat' response has subsided. Then, try again and ask once more whether they are okay.

If they respond again that they are fine, the next step is to tactfully point out what you have observed in their behaviour that has led to your concern. So, for example, you might say, "Well, you say you're fine, but I've noticed that you've seemed very tense and on edge over the past week or so, and that's unlike you." If you tactfully and kindly describe the behaviour that you have seen, then most people will start to open up.

The focus here is on behaviour, not what may be causing the behaviour. What you shouldn't do, under any circumstances, is speculate on the person's psychological or emotional state. For example, it would be a really bad idea to say something like, "I think you might be depressed, and that's making you snappy with everyone." Most of us would find it very intrusive and insensitive to have another person speculate on what we are thinking or feeling. It's perfectly acceptable to comment on observable behaviour, but not to comment on something you can't see and don't understand.

What if this approach doesn't work and the person clams up or perhaps even becomes overtly hostile? In this case, the best approach is to tactfully and gently point out that their behaviour is affecting their work, and maybe even the performance of other people in the team. For example:

> "I've noticed you've been very irritable with colleagues over the past week or so. For example, when Sarah offered to help you yesterday, you told her in a terse manner to go away. That upset Sarah and now other people are wary about talking to you. It's beginning to affect the performance of the whole team. This isn't an acceptable way to behave in the workplace. Please let me know how I can help you with this, or if you don't want any help, please reassure me that this irritability will stop."

This might seem a bit unkind, but often it will lead to the person apologising, explaining what is going wrong for them and asking for support.

How can individuals minimise the risk of burnout?

Think back to when you were last on an aeroplane and a member of the cabin crew was making the safety announcement. You would have been told to put on your own oxygen mask first before helping others. The same principle applies in burnout. You can't help anyone else with burnout, if you are burnt out yourself. Gandhi famously said, "Be the change that you wish to see in the world." As well as caring for yourself, it's helpful to model good self-care for others to see. It follows then that the first place to begin when trying to tackle burnout is with yourself. If you can't care for yourself, you won't be any good at caring for others? Here's what the research says about the best individual strategies for preventing burnout.

The boundary between work and home

The best strategy to prevent or reduce burnout is to have a clear boundary between work and home life. When you're at work, work hard. Then, at the end of the day, do your very best to forget work – switch from work mode into home mode. In other words, leave work at work.

Researchers in Germany found that psychological detachment from work during non-work hours as well as the ability to relax and switch off are the best predictors of prevention and recovery from burnout (Hahn et al., 2011; Sonnentag & Fritz, 2007). People who are able to detach from work, relax, pursue hobbies and spend time with friends seem to be immune from burnout. Of course, the converse is also true. If you find it difficult to switch off from work and relax and you have few interests outside of work and few friends, you are at very high risk of burnout.

Resilience and 'antifragile'

Personal resilience, the ability to bounce back from adversity, is often put forward as being the answer and antidote to burnout. But while it is generally a good thing to be resilient, it can also get you into a lot of trouble and in fact be counter-productive. This is one of the arguments put forward by Nassim Nicholas Taleb in his book *Antifragile* (Taleb, 2012).

When we think of resilience, we tend to think of two extremes. At one end, things are fragile, like a china teacup. At the other end, things are resilient or robust, like a hammer. Fragile things break easily when exposed to stress, but robust things can stand up to stress and not change. In other words, people who are 'fragile' are susceptible to burnout, whereas people who are robust are less prone to burnout. However, according to Taleb, things are not quite so simple.

Taleb argues that the real opposite of fragile isn't robustness or resilience, but antifragile. Antifragile is very different from resilience, because people, objects or systems that are antifragile actually get stronger when exposed to external stress, whereas resilient things stay the same, and fragile things just break.

Most things in nature are antifragile. The best example being your own body. If you expose yourself to stress by exercising, you will get stronger. Expose your immune system to stress by taking a vaccine and your immune system gets stronger. However, in order to benefit from stress (to become antifragile) the stress has to be interspersed with rest and recovery. For example, training for a marathon isn't a matter of running for long distances every day. Most marathon training plans mix short runs with occasional long runs, all of which are broken up by rest days which allow the body to recover. If the runner were to run incessantly without breaks, they would get injured and never make it to marathon day.

This is a great metaphor for many people's working lives. They work long hours, miss coffee and lunch breaks and work at weekends. It's hardly surprising that many people burn out.

Being antifragile applies, not just to people but also to bigger systems including organisations.

BOX 4.2 HOW BEING RESILIENT CAN HURT YOU

On 26 March 2016, the boxer Nick Blackwell fought Chris Eubank Jr at Wembley Stadium. It was a tough fight and both boxers were breathing heavily. By the sixth round, Eubank was clearly winning, but Blackwell always came back for more. No matter how much pressure he was under, he stood there and took it and did his best to fight back. He was the embodiment of resilience.

After ten rounds in the ring, Blackwell had a closed left eye and blood coming from his nose. The match was stopped by the referee. Blackwell was taken to hospital on a stretcher while receiving oxygen. He had suffered a brain bleed.

Blackwell was astounding in his courage and his resilience. But the problem with resilience is that you can only go on for so long. Eventually, the punches get to you, and, like Nick Blackwell, you collapse. If you are a runner, you can only run so far before you eventually stop. It's the same in life and in business. The person, the team and the whole organisation can only tolerate stress for so long until that final punch gets them. Resilience will eventually turn into fragility.

How to become antifragile

If you want to avoid burnout and help others to avoid burnout, you could do a lot worse than organise your life to become antifragile. Here are some ideas for how you might do this:

Develop your awareness

A property of antifragile is the ability to react and adapt quickly to your environment. To be able to do this, you first have to be aware of what is going on around you. So, you should try to become more aware of yourself, other people and your environment.

Everyone today is under tremendous pressure to do their best. It is very easy to get caught up in the hamster wheel of life, simply reacting to whatever is going on around you. When you do this, you miss the subtle clues that help you to adjust more effectively to your environment. These clues might be physical – your shoulders tightening up, for example. The clues might be from other people – when one of your colleagues looks slightly anxious or sad or angry. Being aware of these subtle pieces of evidence is the first step to taking correcting action. If you notice your shoulders are tense, have a stretch and go for a walk. If you notice a colleague is anxious, talk to them about it – invite them to join you for your short walk. If you don't even notice, you don't have a chance to correct it.

Cultivate stress and take breaks

In Chapter 2 I talked about the Yerkes–Dodson curve and how it showed stress creates lots of positive energy. However, it is only good when it is acute. When stress is chronic, it is very bad for you and triggers all kinds of nasty things like high blood pressure, heart disease and of course, burnout. However, short bursts of stress, even very high stress, followed by periods of rest and recovery, makes you stronger. It's like exercise: if you run three times a week, you will get fitter, but if you run every day without any rest periods, you are likely to get injured.

Stress at work is only bad when it is unrelenting – one thing after another, without any recovery time. So, if there is a lot of stress in your life, make sure you build in lots of rest and recovery time. In many jobs where concentration is critical, this is built in. Medical scientists who spot cancer cells on microscope slides have to take regular breaks, otherwise they make errors that can kill. Similarly, lorry drivers must follow rules on how many hours they can drive and the number of breaks they must take.

Antifragile people and systems survive and thrive because of spare capacity. But nowadays, especially in the workplace, there seems to be hardly any spare capacity. Everybody is at full throttle all the time. It sometimes seems like one person is doing the work that would previously have been done by two people. This is all well and good until something goes wrong. Doing the work of two people is exhausting. To be antifragile we sometimes just need to take a break; it's as simple as that.

So, rest really helps – but keep in mind that it can't compensate for a toxic culture at work. In the coming chapters we'll explore the cultural and systemic factors implicated in burnout.

Chapter takeaways

- Obstacles to helping people with burnout include fear of saying the wrong thing, not noticing because you are too busy yourself and worrying that you might appear intrusive.
- Powerful unconscious biases like the bystander effect push us into a default position of turning a blind eye to the early warning signs of burnout.
- To prevent and overcome burnout, maintain a strict boundary between work and home life. Learn to switch off and leave work at work.
- Become antifragile rather than resilient. Build a lot of rest and recovery time into your life.

References

Baim, C., Brookes, S., Mountford, A. & Geese Theatre Company (2002). *The Geese Theatre Handbook : Drama with Offenders and People at Risk.* Winchester, UK: Waterside Press.

Chabris, C. F. & Simons, D. J. (2010). *The Invisible Gorilla : And Other Ways Our Intuitions Deceive Us.* Crown Publishing Group.

Freud, A. (1937). *The Ego and the Mechanisms of Defense.* London: Hogarth Press and Institute of Psycho-Analysis.

Hahn, V. C., Binnewies, C., Sonnentag, S. & Mojza, E. J. (2011). 'Learning How to Recover from Job Stress: Effects of a Recovery Training Program on Recovery, Recovery-Related Self-Efficacy, and Well-Being'. *Journal of Occupational Health Psychology*, 16(2), 202–16. Retrieved from https://doi.org/10.1037/a0022169.

Kahneman, D. (2011). *Thinking, Fast and Slow.* London and New York: Penguin Books.

Lewin, K. (1951). 'Field Theory of Social Science: Selected Theoretical Papers'. Edited by Dorwin Cartwright (pp. xx, 346). New York: Harper & Brothers, 1951. In *The ANNALS of the American Academy of Political and Social Science*, 276(1), 146–7. Retrieved from https://doi.org/10.1177/000271625127600135.

Maister, D. H. (2008). *Strategy and the Fat Smoker: Doing What's Obvious but Not Easy*. Boston: The Spangle Press.

Sanderson, C. (2020). *The Bystander Effect : Understanding the Psychology of Courage and Inaction*. London: Williem Collins.

Sonnentag, S. & Fritz, C. (2007). 'The Recovery Experience Questionnaire: Development and Validation of a Measure for Assessing Recuperation and Unwinding From Work'. *Journal of Occupational Health Psychology*, 12(3), 204–21. Retrieved from https://doi.org/10.1037/1076-8998.12.3.204.

Taleb, N. N. (2012). *Antifragile : Things that Gain from Disorder*. New York: Random House.

Section 2

ROLE

5

BURNOUT AND HOW WORK IS ORGANISED

So far, we've looked at the role that individual and personal factors play in the development of burnout. But what about the job itself? How might the nature of the work and how the work is organised either contribute to or protect you from burnout? One of the key principles in understanding burnout, and one that has been emphasised by the World Health Organization, is that burnout only occurs in the context of work.

In this chapter, we'll take a deep dive into how the nature of work and how work is organised relates to burnout. In particular, we'll explore how the quality of relationships in the workplace plays a pivotal role in both organisational and personal well-being. We'll also look at how unconscious psychological processes within teams and organisations cause much workplace anxiety. Finally, we'll consider a classic case study from the National Health Service that shows how all the above factors can come together to explain why things go wrong in an organisation and how we can put them right.

Jobs, roles and burnout in modern organisations

It's important to understand the underlying processes in teams and organisations that contribute to burnout. Too often, explanations are superficial: it is easy to just say that the individual is weak or there is too much work. These two factors (personal vulnerability and excessive external demand) both contribute to the experience of burnout, but they don't fully explain it. Also, in my experience of working with organisations I have found that these two factors play relatively minor roles when the drama of burnout begins to unfold in the workplace.

In Chapter 2, we started to look at some workplace factors that increase the probability of staff burnout, including poor work–life balance and a lack of clarity about roles and responsibilities. The common theme here is boundaries. The general conclusion of the research is that the clearer these boundaries are, the lower the risk of burnout (Hahn et al., 2011).

Here are some questions that you could ask yourself to clarify the boundaries around your job:

- When does work begin and end?
- When do I start and stop thinking about work?
- What am I responsible for at work and what am I held accountable for?

If you find it hard to answer these questions, maybe you should spend some time reflecting on your relationship with work and whether your job is causing more anxiety than it should. I'm not suggesting that you must be absolutely clear in your answers to the above. Our relationship with work isn't black and white. But you should at least be able to respond to the questions with a "well, most of the time..." type of answer. If you can't, then you may find that an unhealthy culture at work is becoming embodied in you. In other words, something that is outside you (organisational culture) is slowly becoming something that is inside you.

When poor organisational structures become embodied in individual lives, people get ill. The process is an insidious one, where we internalise bad ways of working and enact them in our life outside of work. A toxic organisational culture can really get under our skin to the point that it becomes a part of us.

BOX 5.1 HOW ORGANISATIONAL CULTURES GET UNDER OUR SKIN

The Holocaust wasn't perpetrated by monsters but by ordinary people. That was the conclusion of Hannah Arendt in her book *Eichmann in Jerusalem: A Report on the Banality of Evil* (Arendt, 1994). Adolf Eichmann was in charge of implementing the Final Solution – the Holocaust. Before standing trial, Eichmann was subject to a battery of psychological evaluations administered by six different psychologists. The results indicated that he wasn't insane and he didn't have a personality disorder, but in fact he was a highly conscientious, extroverted and agreeable person. His personality was found to be rather sycophantic; he took pride in doing a good job, and he wanted to be seen to be doing well and be promoted. Eichmann was ambitious, a rule-follower and a bureaucrat who could get the job done. In many respects, then, he was a model employee and the ideal corporate citizen.

Eichmann was, arguably, far removed from the face-to-face murders of the Holocaust. What about those who actually carried out the murders, who herded people into cattle trucks, shoved them into gas chambers, pulled the trigger? What sort of people were they? Well, no doubt some of them were sadists, psychopaths and monsters; but most were ordinary people just doing as they were told and not thinking about things too deeply.

In his book *Ordinary Men*, Christopher Browning describes a group of such people (Browning, 1992). The 'ordinary men' were a volunteer reserve police battalion in rural Germany, rather like our special constables or police community support officers. They weren't professional police; they were postmen, tailors, businessmen and shopkeepers – people just like us. Most of them were in late middle-age and thus had grown up and matured in a pre-Nazi Germany. They weren't young, fanatical Nazis.

The Nazi high command had underestimated the manpower needed to enact the Final Solution. In particular, they hadn't quite grasped how scattered the Jewish population was in Poland; many lived in small rural villages. To boost manpower, they decided to draft in the reserve police battalion. The 'ordinary men' were deployed to Poland. Their task was to round up women and children from small, often remote Polish villages and execute them (the Jewish men had already been rounded up and sent off to work in concentration camps).

(Continued)

Because members of the battalion were middle-aged volunteers, they were given the option not to participate in the executions and just help to round up the victims. However, most chose to take part in the killings because they did not want to let their colleagues down – to let their comrades do all the dirty work. They also felt an obligation to comply with what was being asked of them because they believed that obedience to authority was important and was the right thing to do. The author and academic Daniel Goldhagen's study of the Holocaust argued that this brutality wasn't only the result of the ordinary camaraderie, but an ingrained German anti-Semitism that dated back well into the previous century (Goldhagen, 1997). Again, an example of how culture and belief gets under the skin of 'ordinary' people and influencing them to behave in a manner that might seem superficially incompressible.

The accounts show that many members of the battalion found this work highly traumatising, and many began drinking heavily in an attempt to blot out the horror. But the fact remains that these 'ordinary men' did as they were told and marched women and children into a field, ordered them to lie down, placed their bayonet at the back of the head by the top of the spine and pulled the trigger.

The conclusion of both Arendt's and Browning's scholarly research was that it was ordinary Germans – 'ordinary men' – who made the Holocaust happen. It was people like us who rounded up millions of Jews and systematically shot them in forests, valleys and ditches, or pushed them into cattle trucks and guarded them on their way to the gas chambers of Auschwitz, Dachau and Belsen.

There is a whole genre of research in social psychology that studies how ordinary, 'normal' people can do the most terrible things In the early 1970s, researchers established a pretend prison in the basement of Stanford University to study how people related to each other in a prison situation (Haney et al., 1973). These 1970s' students were randomly assigned the roles of guards or prisoners. The experiment had to be stopped after a few days because the 'guards' began to take their role a little too seriously and started to behave in a very authoritarian and sometimes sadistic manner. Similarly, 'prisoners' became passive, anxious and depressed. Remember, both 'prisoners' and 'guards' were randomly selected from the same population. The only factor that was different was the organisational role they were assigned.

This research was designed to show that many acts of cruelty and brutality aren't carried out by monsters but by so-called normal people.

It also illustrates how easily organisational values and culture become internalised in individual personal behaviour.[1]

Why is this relevant to burnout? Well, if the organisation culture is one of overwork, lack of compassion and lack of integrity, then sooner or later these aspects of the culture will be internalised by many people who work within that organisation: they'll overwork, they won't be compassionate and they will ignore the need for integrity.

The work by Arendt, Browning and Zimbardo is terrifying because it shows that it's not as difficult as you might think for an organisational culture to seduce normal people into behaving like monsters. The culture of the organisation becomes the belief system of the individual. If we accept this, then getting people to work in ways that cause burnout is a doddle. This is why burnout is an organisational issue as well as a personal experience of misery.

Systems and subsystems at work

Let's assume that the job you do is relatively congruent with your personality but you struggled to answer the questions in the preceding section. The next step we could take in finding out why you feel anxious at work is to look at your role as being a small part in a complex system. Organisations are complex systems but they function on basic principles.

Open systems theory was developed back in the 1960s by two psychologists at the Tavistock Institute of Human Relations to better understand how organisations function (Miller & Rice, 1967). Open systems theory refers simply to the concept that organisations are more strongly influenced than we think, by their environment. This includes other organisations, economic, political and social forces as well as the resources the organisation needs to survive.

At its simplest, an organisation is a big rectangular box in which a version process takes place. Inputs come into one end of the box and are converted, and outputs emerge at the other end. In a shoe factory, leather enters the box and is transformed by shoemakers, and shoes emerge at the other end. Essentially, organisations create value by transforming inputs into more valuable outputs. You can think of hospitals like this, with sick people arriving in admissions and well people being discharged. Professional service organisations transform problems and information into solutions. Miller and Rice called this transformational processing the 'primary task' of the organisation. The primary task is the thing the organisation has to do in order to survive.

However, as with all things in life, this is not as simple as it first sounds, because within any organisation there exist different definitions of the primary task. For example, if we think of a shoe factory, the primary task of the chief executive might be to keep the shareholders happy by maximising profits. The chief executive believes that to do this the shoe factory needs to minimise costs and maximise speed of production.

However, the primary task of one of the factory's master shoemakers might be to make the best quality shoe possible, this requires the best and most expensive materials and time. These primary tasks of the CEO and shoemaker are incompatible. You get the point? Already we have two competing primary tasks within the small shoe factory. It is these competing primary tasks that lead to conflict. We tend not to experience this conflict as 'a conflict between subsystems'; we experience it as a personal conflict with Philip in the accounts department or our unreasonable line manager/direct report.

This model was later developed to include concepts from psychoanalysis and group relations (Cardona, 2020). Psychoanalysis sheds light on unconscious processes both within the individual and in teams and organisations. It recognises that many of our behaviours and emotions at work are driven by forces that are not immediately conscious to us.

For example, your relationship with your boss is likely to be coloured by your earlier relationships with authority figures. If, let's say, your parents were strict and authoritarian during your early formative years (birth to five years old), then the chances are that irrespective of their actual behaviours, you will experience your line manager as being strict and authoritarian. And if your boss is a kind and permissive type, you might behave in ways that provoke authoritarian behaviour from them.

Psychoanalysis also brings the concept of defence mechanisms to understanding our behaviour within organisations. For example, when we feel anxiety, we can cope with this in various ways. We can deny that the problem that is causing the anxiety exists or is a serious problem. We can in effect turn a blind eye to it. Another common workplace defence mechanism is projection – in other words, blaming somebody else when something goes wrong.

These unconscious defence mechanisms occur in groups of people as well as individuals. The psychoanalyst Wilfred Bion, who studied group dynamics, coined the term 'anti-task' to describe activities that are unconscious avoidance of the real work that needs to be done (Bion, 1990). For example, having yet another planning meeting, rather than just getting on with things. In effect, the superfluous planning meeting sabotages the real work task.

Bion said that groups, or teams at work, can be in one of two modes: work task mode (getting on with the task) or anti-task mode (avoiding the work task). In work task mode, the team feels energetic, creative and effective. It is doing what it is supposed to be doing. In anti-task mode, the team has a different purpose. For example, say one team member has an idea that all the other team members just know is not going to work. Rather than tell that person kindly but firmly that their idea is a non-runner, the team struggles to get through the agenda and puts off the decision to the next meeting. This may be to avoid hurting the feelings of the person whose idea it was, or just to avoid the discomfort of dealing with an opinionated or loud group member. From the outside, the team looks like it's doing a lot of productive work, but actually it's avoiding the real work. This is what Wilfred Bion would describe as anti-task behaviour.

Bion identified three 'unconscious traps' that teams sometimes fall into:

- *Dependency*: when the team becomes over-dependent on the leader. It feels like the team loses all of its skills, experience and capacity for independent thought, leaving just the leader with all the responsibility. This can be initially seductive for all concerned. The leader feels important and the team can sit back and relax. But after a while, the team ends up feeling useless and de-skilled and the leader feels isolated, put upon and anxious.
- *Pairing*: this is similar to dependency. In this trap, the team abdicates their responsibility not to the leader but to two other team members, who as a pair discuss a decision while the rest of the team passively look on, letting them get on with it.
- *Fight or flight*: this happens when the team gets caught up in 'fighting' an external enemy rather than getting on with the job. This can be

seen most clearly in the development of organisational silos, where the performance of the business becomes secondary to not being pushed around by those idiots in (for example) sales and marketing, finance or compliance.

All of these processes and traps (defence mechanisms) reduce anxiety in the short term, but they always rebound to cause conflict in the long term. These conflicts cause stress and anxiety, and can lead to burnout.

The dominance hierarchy

Let's return to the issue of burnout. Where you fit in the pecking order has a big impact on your susceptibility to burnout.

The systems and subsystems described in the preceding section are experienced as a hierarchy, or management structure. Everybody in an organisation has a line manager (perhaps with the exception of the CEO, although even the CEO reports to the board) and many people have direct reports. We all have a place in the pecking order of corporate life. We all have differing levels of status in the organisation.

The Canadian clinical psychologist and author Jordan Peterson has written about how contemporary human systems such as management hierarchies are forms of the dominance hierarchy.[2] In his book *The 12 Rules for Life: An Antidote to Chaos* (Peterson, 2018), he describes how hierarchy emerged way back in our phylogenetic tree and can be seen in all human and animal groups. Ants have a dominance hierarchy, as do birds and apes. Peterson notes that all human groups and organisations have dominance hierarchies, from the church to the National Health Service, and even the British Labour Party. He famously argued that lobsters, which have been around for about 800 million years, use similar neurochemical systems to human beings to track their social position in relation to other lobsters: a high-status lobster, like a high-status human, will have higher levels of serotonin compared to a lobster further down in the pecking order. This translates in both animals and humans into greater calm, confidence and subjective well-being. All of these properties are important in determining our vulnerability, or not, to burnout. Peterson argues that it's important to understand our own actions, motivations and behaviours in the context of our existence within the dominance hierarchy.

Similarly, in his book *The Status Syndrome* Michael Marmot links status to well-being (Marmot, 2015). He shows convincingly that your health, your level of contentment with life and even how long you live are overwhelmingly determined by one factor: status. Forget things like income or education; status has, by far, the biggest influence on your health, sense of well-being and longevity.

Status simply means your importance relative to others, or in other words, where you are in the pecking order. Or, where you are in the dominance hierarchy.

The importance of status has its roots in our hunter-gatherer past. When we as a species were evolving, our relative position in the social group to which we belonged could be a matter of life and death. It determined our access to food, safety and a mate. Because this was so important for survival, evolution equipped us with brain circuits that constantly monitor our status relative to others. Even in trivial situations like having a brief conversation with another person, deep in your brain there will be an awareness of your status relative to the other person. This phenomenon was famously described by George Bernard Shaw in his play *Pygmalion* when he wrote, "*It is impossible for an Englishman to open his mouth without making some other Englishman hate or despise him*" (Shaw, 1916). He makes the point that accent is a marker of social and economic class – or in other words, status.

The brain thinks about status like it thinks about numbers. Your sense of status goes up when you feel superior to another person. The brain's reward centre is stimulated and pleasure-inducing chemicals flood your nervous system. One piece of research found that an increase in perceived status was similar in strength to a financial windfall (Izuma et al., 2008). Winning a game or an argument probably feels good because of the perception of increased status and the resulting activation of the brain's reward and pleasure centres.

As you might expect, the opposite is also true. Your sense of status goes down when you feel inferior to the other person. This generates a strong threat response and an activation of the freeze, fight or flight response. The brain's centres that register physical pain are very close to and share some circuits with the centres that register emotional or social pain. That is why we experience feelings as physical bodily sensations. When someone is nasty to us, we talk about it being a 'kick in the guts'. A loss of status hurts.

Daily burnout experiences

The quality of relationships at work influences how happy or stressed you feel. If you talk to anybody at work who is feeling stressed and anxious, they will probably tell you that they have good days and bad days. Just as there are degrees of susceptibility to burnout in the general population, there is much variation in how bad a person might feel from day to day. Burnout isn't caused by one big event; rather, it happens during the course of thousands of day-to-day workplace experiences.

A Swiss study found, unsurprisingly, that the more negative interactions people had with others during a day, the more they experienced fatigue. Interestingly, the study also found that positive interactions with people only resulted in subjects feeling better when those positive interactions took place in the context of a chronically stressful environment. In other words, if your workplace is generally good natured and someone pays you a compliment, that won't have much impact on your well-being. However, if you work in a really negative, unpleasant environment and someone pays you a compliment, that will result in a significant alleviation of your stress levels (Gross et al., 2011).

Day-to-day experiences of incivility and rudeness grind people down and ultimately lead to burnout (Rahim & Cosby, 2016). This makes intuitive sense, but can we quantify the impact of incivility on performance and creativity? Christine Porath and Amir Erez from the University of Southern California devised a clever and illuminating piece of research to answer this question. In the study, one group of participants witnessed rudeness and a second group actually experienced being treated rudely. A third group (control group) neither witnessed nor was subjected to rudeness. All the three groups were then asked to complete some problem-solving and creativity exercises. The group who had been treated rudely found it hard to focus on the tasks. Their performance was 61 per cent worse than the group who hadn't encountered any rudeness, and they produced less than half as many ideas in the creativity test. However, what was really interesting was that in the group who merely *witnessed* rudeness to another person, their problem solving was 33 per cent worse and they came up with 39 per cent fewer creative ideas. Porath and Erez also found that when people were exposed to incivility, they were far less inclined to help others: 73 per cent of those who hadn't experienced rudeness would volunteer to help someone, but this fell to only 24 per cent in those who had been treated rudely (Porath & Erez, 2007).

How the fledgling NHS tackled burnout in nursing students

The theories I have described in this chapter might seem a bit abstract and academic. However, all of them have been applied to improve organisational efficiency and well-being in many organisations. One of the best examples of how this approach has transformed an organisation is Isabel Menzies Lyth's work with the NHS (Menzies, 1960).

The National Health Service was born on the 5 July 1948. This creation was a fantastic achievement by the post-war Labour government. However then, as now, funding the NHS was a problem, with actual costs far exceeding projected costs.

By the late 1950s, King's College Hospital, a large teaching hospital in London, was in the midst of a staffing crisis. Much of the basic frontline nursing care was carried out by student nurses, but they were leaving the profession in droves. When asked why, many said that they had entered the nursing profession to care for people, but these expectations weren't generally met. The nurses complained that they didn't have much meaningful time with individual patients and they found the work to be both exhausting and unrewarding.

There was also conflict within the senior clinical staff and hospital managers. The clinical staff responsible for teaching complained about the pressure in combining staffing needs and training needs. The hospital mangers were terrified that the poor retention of the students would result in a complete breakdown in staffing levels and the ability of the hospital to provide care.

A way had to be found to reduce attrition by reconciling the need for student nurses to carry out the practical, sometimes mundane nursing tasks, while at the same time meeting the nurse's need for job satisfaction.

In an attempt to find a solution, the hospital sought help from a young psychoanalyst and organisational consultant called Isabel Menzies.

In the autumn and winter of 1959, she undertook a piece of research and consultancy at King's College Hospital that helped them to resolve this dilemma. The research gave birth to a paper that has become a classic in organisational theory, group dynamics and indeed psychoanalysis. The paper focused on the structure of the hospital nursing service and how the hospital's way of organising the work had a direct and powerful impact on levels of anxiety and job satisfaction experienced by the student nurses.

Although Menzies didn't directly discuss burnout, her findings are very relevant to understanding how the way in which work is organised can either result in burnout (in this case students leaving the nursing profession) or efficiency and job satisfaction.

Menzies recognised the fundamental ambivalence in nursing. On the one hand, nurses want to care for people and develop good relationships with them. On the other hand, this brings a lot of anxiety and pain. Much nursing involves doing things that people usually find personal and often disturbing and disgusting – like dealing with emotional distress, nakedness and bodily functions. It also involves the risk of becoming close to and fond of the patient, who might be suffering, in great pain or even dying. Menzies hypothesised that in order to protect hospital staff from these painful feelings, unconscious defensive systems had gradually evolved in the hospital. These included:

- **Focusing on the task, not the patient**: rather than one nurse looking after a number of patients, nurses would be given tasks to do across the ward. So one nurse might take the temperature of every patient, and another would go around and do the blood pressures. This breakdown of labour minimised the chances of any one individual nurse becoming attached to any one individual patient.
- **Depersonalisation and subtle dehumanisation of the patients**: rather than referring to the patient by name – 'Mr Robinson in bed five' – patients were referred to by their condition. Mr Robinson became 'the diabetic in bed five'.
- **Detachment from and denial of feelings**: the student nurses were explicitly told not to get attached to patients and not to discuss their

emotions at work. Menzies observed nurses being angrily told off for feeling upset rather than being supported.

- **Lack of individual responsibility and control**: the hospital procedures minimised nurses feeling individual responsibility and control by involving as many staff as possible in decisions, then having decisions checked and rechecked, and finally putting off making decisions until as late as possible.
- **Collusive redistribution of responsibility and irresponsibility**: a blame culture evolved to attribute responsibility to other groups. Menzies observed the students habitually complaining that other types of nurses were irresponsible. The complaints were often about categories of nurses rather than individual nurses.

Whilst this unconscious way of organising the work protected the nursing staff from the anxieties associated with the work, it also cut them off from the rewards and satisfaction of getting to know individual patients and developing an appropriate attachment to them. It was this that was driving the lack of work satisfaction and staff attrition.

Menzies' work led to a fundamental change in how people are nursed, not only at King's College Hospital, but nationally. Nowadays, if you are unfortunate enough to end up in hospital, you will most likely be looked after in a bay with four or five other patients. You are likely to have a named nurse who will be responsible for most of your care. You will hopefully be treated as an individual and not just 'the diabetic in bed five'.

When hospital systems don't take account of the defence mechanisms that Menzies identified, it often results in catastrophe. The Mid Staffordshire Hospital scandal is a good example. Between 400 and 1,200 patients died as a result of poor care between January 2005 and March 2009 at this district general hospital in Staffordshire (Campbell, 2013). The reasons for this disaster were complex, but it is certainly possible to see how the actions identified by Menzies 60 years before contributed to the death of patients. There was a focus on the tasks of nursing (and indeed healthcare) to the exclusion of individual patients; a subtle dehumanisation of patients where they were regarded as problems rather than human beings; detachment and denial of feelings by the staff; and attribution of responsibility when things went wrong (in other words, everybody wanted to cover their own backs).

Chapter takeaways

- Organisations are systems that transform 'raw' inputs into valuable outputs. This is the primary task of the organisation; it's what it has to do in order to survive.
- Confusion about what the primary task is and who is responsible for what creates stress, which leads to anxiety and burnout.
- The culture of an organisation can get under our skin and influence our feelings and behaviour.
- We exist in a dominance hierarchy and our position has a big impact on our sense of well-being.
- Organisations have a conscious and unconscious life.

Notes

1 There are many other social psychology studies that show just how willing people are to commit evil. One of the most famous is Stanley Milgram's research on obedience to authority. A contemporary documentary about the research can be seen on YouTube: https://www.youtube.com/watch?v=fCVlI-_4GZQ
2 He adapts the term dominance hierarchy to *competence hierarchy*, feeling that this better reflects how the dominance hierarchy works in human systems.

References

Arendt, H. (1994). *Eichmann in Jerusalem: A Report on the Banality of Evil*. New York: Penguin Books.

Bion, W. R. (1990). *Experiences in Groups*. Abingdon: Routledge.

Browning, C. R. (1992). *Ordinary Men : Reserve Police Battalion 101 and the Final Solution in Poland*. New York: HarperCollins.

Campbell, D. (2013). 'Mid Staffs hospital scandal: the essential guide'. *Guardian*, 6 April. Retrieved from https://www.theguardian.com/society/2013/feb/06/mid-staffs-hospital-scandal-guide#maincontent.

Cardona, F. (2020). *Work Matters: Consulting to Leaders and Organizations in the Tavistock Tradition*. Abingdon: Routledge.

Goldhagen, D. J. (1997). *Hitler's Willing Executioners: Ordinary Germans and the Holocaust*. London: Abacus.

Gross, S., Semmer, N. K., Meier, L. L., Kälin, W., Jacobshagen, N., & Tschan, F. (2011). 'The Effect of Positive Events at Work on After-work Fatigue: They Matter Most in Face of Adversity'. *Journal of Applied Psychology*, 96(3), 654–64. Retrieved from https://doi.org/10.1037/a0022992.

Hahn, V. C., Binnewies, C., Sonnentag, S. & Mojza, E. J. (2011). 'Learning How to Recover from Job Stress: Effects of a Recovery Training Program on Recovery, Recovery-Related Self-Efficacy, and Well-Being'. *Journal of Occupational Health Psychology*, 16(2), 202–16.

Haney, C., Banks, C. & Zimbardo, P. (1973). 'Interpersonal Dynamics in a Simulated Prison'. *International Journal of Criminology & Penology*, 1(1), 69–97.

Izuma, K., Saito, D. N. & Sadato, N. (2008). 'Processing of Social and Monetary Rewards in the Human Striatum'. *Neuron*, 58(2), 284–94. Retrieved from https://doi.org/10.1016/j.neuron.2008.03.020.

Marmot, M. (2015). *Status Syndrome: How Your Social Standing Directly Affects Your Health*. London: Bloomsbury Paperbacks.

Menzies, I. E. P. (1960). 'A Case-Study in the Functioning of Social Systems as a Defence against Anxiety'. *Human Relations*, 13(2), 95–121. Retrieved from https://doi.org/10.1177/001872676001300201.

Miller E. J. & Rice, A. K. (1967). *Systems of Organization: Task and Sentient Systems and Their Boundary Control*. London: Tavistock Publications.

Peterson, J. B. (2018). *12 Rules for Life: An Antidote to Chaos*. London: Allen Lane.

Porath, C. L. & Erez, A. (2007). 'Does Rudeness Really Matter? The Effects of Rudeness on Task Performance and Helpfulness'. *Academy of Management Journal*, 50(5), 1181–97. Retrieved from https://doi.org/10.5465/amj.2007.20159919.

Rahim, A. & Cosby, D. M. (2016). 'A Model of Workplace Incivility, Job Burnout, Turnover Intentions, and Job Performance'. *Journal of Management Development*, 35(10), 1255–65. Retrieved from https://doi.org/10.1108/JMD-09-2015-0138.

Shaw, B. (1916). *Pygmalion*. New York: Brentano.

6

PREVENTING AND MINIMISING THE RISK OF BURNOUT IN OTHERS

In this chapter, I suggest a new way to think about burnout. I also offer you some practical tools that you can use to minimise the risk of burnout in people you lead, manage and work with. Of course, these tips also apply to you.

Previously, I talked about how burnout happens in systems. Within every system there are lots of subsystems. You are likely to work in one of the subsystems and have varying degrees of influence about how things work within that subsystem. You might be a leader, manager or supervisor, or you might just be someone who works there. However much influence you have, there are things you can do to make life a bit better and minimise the stresses that lead to burnout.

All of the ideas and tips in this chapter seek to make you and the people you work with more antifragile. In other words, you'll not only cope better with the stresses of day-to-day life, but actually grow and become stronger as a result of those stresses.

Burnout and energy

We can think of well-being and its opposite, burnout, in terms of energy. Well-being is an abundance of energy within a person or a team. When you are feeling energetic, you're enthusiastic, alert and up for a challenge. Conversely, when your energy levels are depleted, you feel physically tired, lacking enthusiasm and mentally exhausted. The three essential criteria that define burnout are exhaustion, detachment/cynicism and impaired work performance. All of these criteria are another way of describing depleted levels of energy.

BOX 6.1 THE TEAM AS A BATTERY

Earlier this year, I was asked to coach the new CEO of a failing technology company. I was told that this was a young, funky start-up company that should be doing well, but wasn't. Unfortunately, the owner of the company had appointed one of his best friends to be CEO, and this person wasn't coping at all well.

I arrived early and was asked to wait in the corner of the swish, brightly decorated open-plan office. The room was filled with young people dressed very casually – the typical tech company. But everybody looked fed up. This roomful of young, energetic people should have been buzzing with activity, but instead the atmosphere felt dead, like a black cloud was hanging over the room. I eventually saw the CEO, who didn't feel that he needed coaching, believing that the failure was due to "all the idiots I'm surrounded with". So nothing came of it in the end.

However, I learned something by reflecting on that experience. Organisations and teams are like batteries – stores of human energy. If the organisation and team are fully charged, then performance will be great and the atmosphere will crackle with excitement and energy. But if the organisation's and team's batteries are flat, then performance will be poor, as in the tech company.

The four types of energy

When we think about our energy, we tend to focus only on physical energy. However, there are four sources that contribute to our overall energy levels.

Physical energy

In the 17th century, the philosopher Rene Descartes argued that the mind and body are distinct and separable (Russell, 1945). This view persists, and it is not overly helpful in understanding burnout, which is still viewed by many as a 'mental' problem that is solved through an intellectual answer, such as a talking therapy. However, the experience of burnout is both physical *and* mental. It does include mental aspects, such as cynicism, but the factors that overwhelmingly dominate the experience of burnout are physical ones. People suffering burnout feel exhausted, anxious and detached from life. All of these are embodied physical experiences that represent a decrease in physical energy.

One of the problems with burnout is that it easily becomes a vicious circle of physical exhaustion. You work long hours and get tired. Your concentration decreases and it takes you longer to complete a given task. Therefore, in order to complete your work, you have to work even longer hours – and so it goes on.

Emotional energy

If you feel fed up, unappreciated or constantly stressed and worried, your emotional energy levels will be low and your work performance is likely to be correspondingly low. Our emotional energy is pretty much determined by the quality of our relationships. It's difficult to focus on anything or get things done if your workplace is negative and dominated by office politics.

According to research, even witnessing incivility at work upsets most people and significantly impairs performance. Psychologists Christine Porath and Amir Erez devised an experiment where one group of participants witnessed rudeness, another group actually experienced being treated rudely and a third group encountered no rudeness at all. The groups were then asked to complete problem-solving and creativity tasks. The group who had been treated rudely found it hard to focus on the tasks and their performance plummeted. Compared to the group who hadn't encountered any rudeness, their problem-solving ability was 61 per cent worse and they produced less than half as many ideas in the creativity test. In the group who just witnessed rudeness, their problem solving was 33 per cent worse and they came up with 39 per cent fewer creative ideas. The psychologists also found that when people encounter incivility, they are far less inclined to help others. They found that 73 per cent of those who hadn't experienced rudeness would volunteer to help someone, but this fell to only 24 per cent in those who had been treated rudely (Porath & Erez, 2007).

For our emotional energy levels to recharge, we need to work in an environment where we feel respected, appreciated and valued. There is a lot of research in the field of positive psychology that shows how you can do this (Lopez & Snyder, 2011).

Mental energy

This is our ability to focus and concentrate – in other words, our cognitive ability or ability to think. Some work environments support our ability to think, while others disable it. If you're a leader or a manager, you essentially get paid to think. But in many work environments it is very difficult to think clearly. There are so many interruptions in modern open-plan offices, including emails, phone calls and colleagues wanting to talk. The American academic Cal Newport has talked about how the rise of modern technology in the office has sabotaged our ability to concentrate. In his book *Deep Work* (Newport, 2016) he describes work as being either deep or shallow.

Deep work is made up of professional activities performed in a state of distraction-free concentration that push cognitive abilities to their limit. Deep work is valuable, it doesn't happen that much in the modern world and it is meaningful. This is similar to the positive psychology idea of flow (Csikszentmihalyi, 1990), in which a person performing an activity is fully immersed in the task and feels energised and focused. Flow happens when you are completely absorbed in what you are doing. It is very difficult to get into this mindset in most workplaces.

In contrast, shallow work is made up of repetitive, non-demanding tasks that a person can perform easily even when distracted. This work doesn't add much value and is easy to replicate.

Newport argues that years of exposure to shallow work and distractions have a long-lasting, negative impact on our ability to concentrate and focus our attention for more than short periods of time. He talks about how influential and very productive people, such as Carl Jung, Woody Allen and Bill Gates, have removed themselves from distractions in order to produce their enormous and extraordinary body of work. If you are a leader or manager, much of your time at work should be used to engage in work. Unfortunately, the work environment often gets in the way of this.

BOX 6.2 MAKING TIME TO THINK

When Gerry Robinson joined Granada as CEO, it posted a pre-tax loss of £110 million. He turned this around to a profit of £735 million. Robinson attributed his business success to being able to carve out time and space to think, away from the noisy office where you are constantly interrupted. He said:

> Even when I was in full-time employment it was pretty rare for me to be there on Friday afternoons. Unless there was a takeover or something going on, I would switch off completely, particularly if I could absorb myself in one of my hobbies such as painting or playing golf. And always leave firm instructions not to be disturbed.
>
> (Robinson, 2004)

Existential (or spiritual) energy

The greatest source of energy is having an awareness of the meaning and purpose of your job. It's important to really understand why you do what you do and why your work is important and valuable (every job has meaning and dignity). If you feel that what you do is meaningless for you, then every day is going to be a struggle.

There is an old story about three stonemasons in 10th-century Paris. Each of them is asked what they are doing. The first replies that they are carving stone to make a living. The second stonemason talks about the pride he takes in carving beautiful ornamental stonework. The third looks up and says that he is building a cathedral to the glory of God. This story is a bit clichéd, but it makes a good point. The codebreakers at Bletchley Park worked long hours without complaint, because they knew that their work saved lives. If you believe, like the third stonemason or the Bletchley Park codebreakers, that your work has real meaning, then you're far less likely to suffer burnout.

BOX 6.3 VIKTOR FRANKL AND MAN'S SEARCH FOR MEANING

On an autumn day in September 1942, Viktor Frankl, a Jewish psychiatrist, was arrested in Vienna along with his wife and his parents and transported to Auschwitz. By 1945 his family, including his wife, had perished. Frankl managed somehow to survive. The following year he wrote one of the most profound books to be written about the Holocaust and the human condition, *Man's Search for Meaning* (Frankl, 1962). Frankl concluded that the overwhelming difference between those who survived the death camps and those who did not was the person's ability to find meaning and purpose in even the most hopeless circumstances. He wrote:

> Everything can be taken from a man but one thing, the last of the human freedoms – to choose one's attitude in any given set of circumstances, to choose one's own way... Striving to find meaning in one's life is the primary motivational force of man.

Frankl's idea about actively choosing one's attitude to a bad situation is an important one. Doing this helps to remove the sense of meaninglessness that contributes to burnout. It is easy to complain and whine about work, but that usually does not help. If you are doing a meaningful job, remember what that meaning is. If you can't find any meaning in your job, remember why you are doing it – perhaps to provide for your family, or to earn money to allow you to do other, more pleasant and interesting things in your life. Focusing on the meaning of your job, why you do it, really will help you to feel better about a poor situation.

How you can increase the energy in your team and decrease the risk of burnout

Here are some suggestions about how you can increase the energy levels in your team:

Increasing physical energy

This is the easiest, most straightforward and probably most obvious way of improving energy in the team. Here are a few suggestions:

- **Boundaries**: have clear boundaries at work. For example, do your best to enforce start and finish times. Discourage people from coming into the office too early or working late.
- **Regular breaks**: encourage those you manage to take their allocated breaks. Make sure they have their lunch and coffee/tea breaks. Of course, one of the best ways to do this is by setting an example and taking breaks yourself.
- **Physical activity**: start a lunchtime physical activity group. For example, you could organise a walking group to go for a brisk half-hour walk.
- **Exercise**: if you have the resources and authority, set up a workplace gym. If that isn't possible, perhaps you could provide a subsidised company gym membership scheme.
- **Nutrition**: evaluate the food on sale in the staff restaurant. Do you have healthy, nutritious options?
- **Home working**: would some of your staff prefer to work from home for part of the working week?

Increasing emotional energy

The American psychologist Dr John Gottman is probably the world's leading expert on marriage and relationships. After spending 15 minutes with you and your partner, Gottman is able to predict, with 94 per cent accuracy, whether your relationship will be happy and long-lasting, or end up on the rocks. To understand the difference between happy and unhappy couples, Gottman and his colleague Robert Levenson carried out a number of longitudinal studies of married couples in the 1970s. They asked couples to solve a conflict in their relationship in 15 minutes, and then sat back and watched. After carefully reviewing the tapes, they predicted which couples would stay together and which would divorce. Nine years later, they followed up with the couples and found their predictions were over 90 per cent accurate (Gottman & Levenson, 1992).

Gottman and Levenson's discovery was simple. The difference between a happy and unhappy couple is the balance between positive and negative interactions during conflict. There is a very specific ratio that makes love last (Gottman & Silver, 2018). That 'magic ratio' is 5-to-1. This means that for every negative interaction during conflict, a stable and happy marriage has five (or more) positive interactions. On the other hand, unhappy couples engage in fewer positive interactions to compensate for their escalating negativity. If the positive to negative ratio during conflict is 1-to-1 or less, that's unhealthy, and indicates a couple teetering on the edge of divorce.

This is all very interesting, I hear you say, but what has it got to do with work and burnout? Well, the psychologists Marcial Losada and Emily Heaphy wondered if this principle applied to work groups. They studied the performance (financial success, customer satisfaction ratings and 360-degree feedback ratings of team members) of 60 leadership teams at a large IT organisation.

Just like John Gottman with the married couples, they found that the factor that made the greatest difference between the most and least successful teams was the ratio of positive to negative comments that the managers made to one another. The average ratio for the highest-performing teams was 5.6. The medium-performance teams averaged 1.9. The average for the lowest-performing teams was only 0.36 to 1; in other words, almost three negative comments for every positive one (Losada & Heaphy, 2004). This is strong evidence that if you can increase the number of positive to negative interactions in your team, you will reduce the risk of stress and burnout, as well as improving productivity. Oh, and it will make for a nicer place to work.

To increase the emotional energy in your team, actively talk about ways in which you can improve your team's positivity ratio. A great way of doing this is the 'What Went Well' exercise devised by Martin Seligman, founder of the positive psychology movement (Seligman, 2011). At the start of your next team meeting, set aside ten minutes and ask each member to talk about three things that went well over the previous week and why they went well. At first, you will probably find that people look at you blankly and say that they can't remember anything good happening. This is normal, because we tend to have a negativity bias: we focus on the things that have gone wrong, and when things go well, we forget and move on to the next problem, letting our successes fly away like ashes scattered in the wind. If this happens, ask your team to get their diaries out and look back at the previous week. When you do this you will be amazed at how many successes there have been and the immediate uplift in mood when people start sharing them. On the whole, people love talking about their successes and the good things that have happened – they just need a bit of encouragement and a framework within which to do it.

Increasing cognitive energy

In order to increase people's ability to think, focus on what's important and get things done, you need to tell your team to build the following into how they work:

- Work in focused blocks of time (blocks of 90 minutes work well for me). In other words, if you have a piece of work to get done, sit down and focus on that work for this period. Switch off your email notifications, unplug your phone, and either close your office door or put up a 'do not disturb' sign. You will be amazed by how much you can achieve in 90 minutes.
- Between the 90-minute blocks of work, take regular short breaks to refresh and recharge your brain. Get up and go for a walk around, have a cup of coffee or at least have a stretch.
- Get some exercise during the working day. The brain uses massive amounts of oxygen, and simply having a brisk walk once or twice a day really oxygenates the brain and leads to improved cognitive performance (Mandolesi et al., 2018).

Increasing meaning

The most powerful way of increasing energy in a team and decreasing the risk of burnout is to help the people you lead or manage to reconnect with the meaning of their work.

BOX 6.4 RESTORING MEANING IN MEDICINE

Tony is a 46-year-old paediatrician. He is married and has an eight-year-old daughter called Sophie. Tony is a smart, affable, down-to-earth character – he's the sort of doctor who wears a tweed jacket in preference to a dark-blue suit. Until recently, he would have described himself as being tough-minded; he has to be, given the nature of his work. But then came the night his wife came downstairs to find Tony sitting at the kitchen table and sobbing uncontrollably. Next to him was an empty bottle of wine and his laptop, open on a report which told the story of the mistreatment of an eight-year-old child. His life at work had become a blur of meetings, reading and writing reports, and doing his best to support unhappy colleagues. He would see patients, but once he'd carried out an assessment, more junior staff would provide the hands-on treatment. He had become a doctor to help people, but now felt he was just a small cog in the big machine of NHS bureaucracy. Tony was finding it hard to see the meaning of his work anymore.

For all its stress, long hours and poor pay, the one thing that medicine, especially paediatrics, doesn't lack is meaning. Unfortunately, the form-filling, box-ticking bureaucracy of the NHS often puts a barrier between the practitioner and the meaning inherent in the work. In 2018, some colleagues and I were asked to develop a programme to strengthen resilience in medical staff overseeing the safety of children and vulnerable adults. We developed a programme based on the work of Viktor Frankl, which I described earlier (Drayton et al., 2018). Tony's work is difficult and nothing will take away the stress – but connecting with the meaning and importance of the role makes almost any amount of stress bearable.

The American organisational psychologist Adam Grant has spent his career studying meaning and motivation at work. Here are some of his evidence-based ideas for reconnecting people with the meaning of their work (Grant, 2011):

- **Create events where employees can meet customers or service users.** A medical technology company has an annual party in which patients tell salespeople, engineers and technicians how the company's products have transformed their lives. A hospital accident and emergency department organises an annual event at which trauma team members come face to face with people whose lives they saved.
- **Circulate stories that allow employees to learn about their customers' experiences.** The Volvo Saved My Life Club collects videos and letters from drivers whose lives were saved by the company's safety designs.
- **Invite employees to share their own stories.** A bank branch starts weekly team meetings with employees describing memorable instances of helping customers.
- **Turn employees into customers.** A luxury hotel chain invites housekeepers and hotel staff to spend a night in their own hotel.

The problem Tony and so many other people have is that they become caught up in the day-to-day hassles and trivialities of work and forget the real meaning of what they do. We all strive to live a meaningful life and most of us spend a lot of our time at work. Finding or creating meaning at work really helps to avoid burnout.

Chapter takeaways

- Burnout can be thought of as severe and chronic energy depletion.
- There are four categories of personal energy:
  - Physical.
  - Emotional.
  - Cognitive.
  - Spiritual (existential).
- You can increase physical energy with rest, exercise and good diet.
- You can increase emotional energy by building a culture of appreciation and positivity.
- You can increase cognitive energy by decreasing workplace interruptions and encouraging frequent breaks.
- You can increase spiritual energy by reconnecting with the meaning of work.

References

Csikszentmihalyi, M. (1990). *Flow*. New York: Harper and Row.

Drayton, M., Memarzia, J. & Robinson, S. (2018). 'What an Auschwitz Survivor Taught NHS Safeguarding Leads about Resilience'. *The Psychologist*. British Pyschological Society.

Frankl, V. E. (1962). *Man's Search for Meaning: An Introduction to Logotherapy*. (4th ed.). Boston: Beacon Press.

Gottman, J. M. & Levenson, R. W. (1992). 'Marital Processes Predictive of Later Dissolution: Behavior, Physiology, and Health'. *Journal of Personality and Social Psychology*, 63(2), 221–33.

Gottman, J. & Silver, N. (2018). *The Seven Principles for Making Marriage Work*. London: Orion Spring.

Grant, A. M. (2011). 'Motivating Creativity at Work: The Necessity of Others is the Mother of Invention'. *Psychological Science Agenda*, American Psychological Association.

Lopez, S. J. & Snyder, C. R. (eds) (2011). *Oxford Handbook of Positive Psychology*. Oxford: Oxford University Press.

Losada, M. & Heaphy, E. (2004). 'The Role of Positivity and Connectivity in the Performance of Business Teams: A Nonlinear Dynamics Model'. *American Behavioral Scientist*, 47(6), 740–65.

Mandolesi, L., Polverino, A., Montuori, S., Foti, F., Ferraioli, G., Sorrentino, P., & Sorrentino, G. (2018). 'Effects of Physical Exercise on Cognitive Functioning and Wellbeing: Biological and Psychological Benefits'. *Frontiers in Psychology*, 9(509), 27 April. Retrieved from https://doi.org/10.3389/fpsyg.2018.00509.

Newport, C. (2016). *Deep Work: Rules for Focused Success in a Distracted World*. London: Piatkus.

Porath, C. L. & Erez, A. (2007). 'Does Rudeness Really Matter? The Effects of Rudeness on Task Performance and Helpfulness'. *Academy of Management Journal*, 50(5), 1181–97.

Robinson G. (2004). *I'll Show Them Who's Boss*. Harlow: Pearson Education Limited.

Russell, B. (1945). *A History of Western Philosophy*. London: George Allen & Unwin.

Seligman, M. (2011). *Flourish: A New Understanding of Happiness and Well-Being – and How to Achieve Them*. London: Nicholas Brealey Publishing.

7

BURNOUT AND REMOTE WORKING

Working from home has now become a regular part of many people's working life. Following the COVID-19 crisis, many businesses rapidly moved to remote working. Most adapted well to the radically changed business environment. Changes that ordinarily would have taken months to implement happened within weeks.

But what of those working from home? Most people didn't have time to prepare for this massive change to their work and home life. Suddenly, they had to organise and motivate themselves. They had to find somewhere quiet to work, which involved negotiating with their families or others who shared their living space. Remote working was even more stressful for leaders and managers, who had to adapt quickly to leading and managing a remote-working team. It's hard to adapt to novel ways of working, think strategically and motivate people when you are feeling overwhelmed yourself and the main communication tool you have is Zoom.

Remote working can be great. There's no long commute to worry about. You have a lot more flexibility in how you structure your time, and you get to spend more time at home. However, working from home can also have some unpleasant side effects that can increase the risk of burnout.

In this chapter, I explore how remote working can contribute to burnout. I look at how to get the best from working from home, and how best to lead and manage a remote-working team. Finally, I offer some guidance on what to do if things go wrong. All of this is important knowledge, because not only is remote working here to stay, but it's likely to grow and become a routine part of working life for many of us.

Enhanced productivity – but isolation

Most people who work from home work harder than they would in the office. Clare Kelliher and Deidre Anderson studied professional workers and found higher levels of job satisfaction, commitment to work and productivity in those working flexibly from home than those working just at the office (Kelliher & Anderson, 2010). The researchers used social exchange theory (Emerson, 1971) to explain this. The remote worker sees home working and flexibility as a benefit, and 'repays' this benefit with discretionary effort, by working harder. The researchers added that some employers mirror this mindset by regarding flexible working as a benefit that justifies their making unreasonable demands to get a return on their 'generosity'.

This isn't the only research that has found people are more productive when working from home. A study conducted in 2015 by Bloom and colleagues found a 13 per cent improvement in productivity from home workers (Bloom et al., 2015). Another study carried out by Glenn Dutcher found that people are more productive doing challenging, complicated or creative tasks at home (Dutcher, 2012). (When they have to do boring, repetitive or routine tasks, however, their productivity falls, and they would be better in the more structured office environment.)

Unfortunately, the improved productivity of home working comes at a cost. Loneliness and isolation are the biggest problems for people who work remotely. A shocking study by Julianne Holt-Lunstad from Brigham Young University analysed 148 research studies with 308,849 participants on the relationship between loneliness and premature mortality. The study found that social isolation and loneliness significantly increase the risk of premature death by 50 per cent. The magnitude of this effect is comparable with smoking and it exceeds many well-known risk factors such as obesity and physical inactivity (Holt-Lunstad et al., 2010).

The optimal solution that incorporates the benefits of improved productivity and the benefits of social interaction and structure is a hybrid model, with people working from home part of the time with a day or two in the office.

Personality, remote working and burnout

Depending on your personality, working from home can be fantastic or a living hell. In Chapter 3, I discussed how we all have our own unique personality profile. Some of us are extroverted, are open to novel ideas and ways of working, and are agreeable in our dealings with others (to mention just three from the big five model). Others are introverted, don't like change and are disagreeable when asked to do something they don't want to do.

These personality factors have a potent influence on our behaviour, but they don't determine it entirely. To adapt, we learn to change our behaviour. Disagreeable people learn how to compromise, or at least to be more diplomatic in their conversations. More agreeable colleagues learn to be more assertive, even if being assertive makes them feel uncomfortable. This is an important point, because behaving in a manner that doesn't fit with our core personality make-up is exhausting. An extrovert loves giving a presentation because it gives them energy. They get a buzz from it and feel excited afterwards. An introvert can give a similarly good presentation, but will feel anxious during the presentation and drained afterwards.

We have all built up strategies over the years to manage those situations that we find difficult. We have developed our own psychological and emotional scaffolding to support the parts of our personality that lack strength in certain situations. For example, many people who are not very conscientious gravitate to highly structured corporate organisations that help them manage the disorganised and 'lazy' aspects of their personality. They enjoy structure, routines and being told what to do. These rigid structures are like a psychological scaffolding holding the persona together. A good example is the military. This is why some veterans struggle with civilian life, when the military 'scaffolding' is absent.

The problem is that in times of crisis and change our psychological scaffolding gets dismantled. An extroverted person is likely to feel deprived of the social energy that keeps their spirits up when their work-based social life becomes 20 seconds of "How are you?" at the start of each Zoom call. Similarly, an introverted person gets deprived of the 'me time' they need in order to recharge emotionally when they have to attend back-to-back Zoom calls, with no commute in between to be alone with their thoughts and de-stress.

In this way, a person's personality can contribute to the development of burnout when working remotely.

How to get the best from home working and avoid burnout

First of all, put some clear boundaries around your work. Have a proper start and finish time, and develop a disciplined way of managing the day. Have a shower, get dressed and then get started. If you're an extrovert and get your energy from being around others, ensure that happens. Try to plan the day that you would like to have, or you will be at the mercy of other people's plans.

A 'to do' list can be a tyranny, where you never catch up and you feel overwhelmed. Instead, just block out time in your diary with things you need to do – and don't forget to include breaks and exercise time.

Remember to do the things that make working from home enjoyable. Play the music you like, have a nap if you want and focus on the pleasurable things about your situation.

All these are fairly obvious ideas. Let's go a bit deeper now.

Consider your personality

If you want to get the most from working from home, you need to do a bit of self-reflection. Think about the five factors of your personality and the person you are. Are you extroverted – do you get a lot of your energy from being around others? Are you an organised or disorganised person? Are you a worrier or more of a happy-go-lucky, 'everything will turn out fine' sort of person?

The key to having an enjoyable time working from home is self-awareness. Once you've done this self-reflection, you can organise your work time in a way that plays to your strengths and compensates for your weaknesses. This is why a lot of advice you'll see on social media about working from home misses the point. Advice that will be helpful for an extroverted person will be useless if you are an introverted person – in fact, if you follow it, it might make you feel a lot worse. So, you need to start with your personality and pick the advice that fits your personality and your strengths.

Here's an example of what I mean. Let's say you are a conscientious person. You'll find working from home to be a doddle. The enormous danger for you, though, is workaholism. There will be no-one there to notice when you need a break and tell you to go home. So, set some boundaries around your work. Have a specific time to start, break times and a definite finish time – and stick to them. You've probably heard of Parkinson's Law, which says that work expands to fill the time allocated to it.

When you are working, minimise any interruptions. Switch off your email and mobile phone. If you can, only check your email messages maybe three times a day – otherwise leave it switched off. If you do this, you will be amazed how much work you get done.

Remove distractions

In his book *Deep Work*, American academic Cal Newport suggests removing all distractions from your workplace when you are working (Newport, 2016). Switch off your email if you can, or at least switch off the email notifications. I know that in practice many people find this hard – and of course the internet can be a distraction too. If you struggle with this you could try using a distraction blocking app like Freedom (https://freedom. to/dashboard). I use this app and it's extremely effective. You set a list of all the things it should block, like the internet (or certain websites) and email, and then you can run scheduled/timed sessions so that you can focus on your work. The schedule aspect really helps with working for short bursts and taking a break, as you get a notification that the session is ended and this tells you it's time to pause. The same goes for your phone.

Work in short bursts

In *Deep Work*, Newport also recommends structuring your work time into short bursts of activity broken up by rest periods. For example, do half an hour of intense deep work, then have a ten-minute break, and then go back to work for another half an hour.

Leading and managing the remote team

If you feel a bit unsettled about managing a remote-working team situation, you are right to, because leading a remote team differs greatly from leading a team in the office. It requires a different mindset – a distinct way of thinking about how you organise the work and how you manage all relationship issues that may arise.

Here are some practical things you can do to minimise stress and the consequent risk of burnout in remote workers.

Technology

One of the major sources of stress is the technology associated with home working. This may be obvious advice, but I think the place to start is making sure that everybody working from home has got the technology they need and that they know how to use it. You should check this out carefully. Many people don't enjoy asking for help. They think, "If I ask for help, they'll think I'm stupid." So, take the time to make sure all the tech is working and that people understand how to use it.

Once you've done this, consider how you organise your meetings to avoid 'Zoom fatigue'. Recent research by Christoph Riedl and Anita Williams Woolley found that remote teams who communicate in short bursts of activity mixed in with periods of intense individual focus perform far better than teams whose communication is less structured. They called this 'bursty work' (Riedl & Wolley, 2017).

Motivating the remote team

The hardest part of managing a remote team is keeping team members motivated.

Any leader or manager worth their salt knows that change makes employees anxious. Any psychologist worth their salt knows that when people get anxious, they look for support and guidance from authority figures in their life. If you are a manager, that's you!

Now, this can be tough, because you may also feel anxious because of the changes in your working life. The first thing you need to do is protect your employees from your own anxiety. You should find the balance between acknowledging people's worries and providing a positive and hopeful message for the future. It's that balance between acknowledging anxiety and giving hope that is the key to motivation.

Check in

The most important thing you can do to motivate your staff is to be more psychologically and emotionally present for them. This doesn't mean engaging them in interminably long Zoom meetings. Rather, it means just three short updates and check-ins a day. In a very helpful article in the *Harvard Business Review* (Larson et al., 2020), Barbara Larson and colleagues emphasised the importance of establishing scheduled, structured daily check-in meetings for managing remote teams. In addition, they highlighted that clarity of communication about expectations, ways of working and responsibility is essential in managing the remote team.

Set a structure

Another factor that helps people who are feeling anxious is having clear boundaries around their life. They might not be able to predict their long-term future, but if they can at least predict how their day will be, that really helps.

Establish a clear start and finish for the working day at home. For example, you might want to announce when you 'arrive at the office'. At the start of your day, send out a message to say "I'm at work". This lets people know that they can contact you. Similarly, at the end of the working day, let people know you are going home – which is daft really, because you're already at home, but you get my point. This will also give them permission to 'go home'.

Also have prearranged break times. Try to fit these in with flexible working as best you can. The enormous advantage of working from home is being able to work flexibly, maybe starting early in the morning and having a nap in the afternoon (try that at the office!), so arrange breaks to best suit people's needs.

Give positive feedback

Do your best to create a culture of appreciation (Cooperrider & Whitney, 2005). When people are working at home, they get a lot less feedback from their manager. You need to counter this by upping your level of positive feedback for people's work. In fact, I'd advise you to be over-the-top. To use a metaphor, it's like you telling them from a distance they've done well, but because you're at a distance, you need to shout a bit.

Here's a technique you can use from Professor Martin Seligman and the positive psychology movement. Once a week, set aside ten minutes at the start of your team meeting and ask all the members to tell you three things that went well that week. This will help them focus on the positives of the situation rather than the negatives (Seligman, 2011). Most of us have a negativity bias (Kahneman, 2011) and focus on the threats rather than the enjoyable things that have happened. This exercise helps to recalibrate things.

Encourage sociability

Finally, build in some social interaction. Isolation and social disconnection are big problems in remote working. So, as a leader it's important that you encourage opportunities for informal chitchat. This will support team cohesion and a sense of belonging, which otherwise can quickly dissolve in a crisis. Pair people up to have 15-minute online coffee breaks where the only rule is 'no talking about work'. Try to organise some quizzes online, that kind of thing.

What to do if things go wrong

Things can sometimes go wrong with remote working. While most people enjoy working from home and perform better, others seem to flounder.

Those who do not cope with remote working seem to fall into one of two distinct groups:

- They lack motivation and disengage with their job. They struggle to get going and their performance is poor.
- They become overly dependent and seem to lose confidence in their abilities. These folk find it almost impossible to decide what to do and need constant validation of their work.

There is no great secret about managing this. It's the same as managing difficulties in the office. It's hard, and you can't get away from that.

The key to managing difficulties well is good communication. If someone's performance is poor when working at home, talk to them about it. Ask them how things are. Ask them what you can do to help them. They might be experiencing difficulties in their domestic situation. Or they might be the sort of person who just needs a lot of structure in their work life.

Another reason for poor performance is that the person is experiencing problems with their mental health. In Chapter 2, I described what to look out for in people who are struggling with mental health problems, the obstacles to helping and what you can do to help. It's just the same if you suspect one of your remote workers might be struggling with their mental health. The primary difference is that you will communicate with them over Zoom or telephone rather than face to face. This will result in much of the subtlety and nuance of the conversation being lost. You won't be able to observe body language. So, bear this in mind when talking to the person you have concerns about. It might be easier to have this conversation using the telephone rather than video calling.

If you have done everything you can to help the person who is performing poorly, remember that just because the person is working from home, that doesn't excuse them from your company's performance-management policies and procedures. So, if the person doesn't have any reasons for their poor performance, then it becomes a straightforward performance-management issue.

What about the leader?

The last thing I want to talk about is how you, as a leader, can manage your own well-being when working remotely. Catherine Sandler at the Tavistock

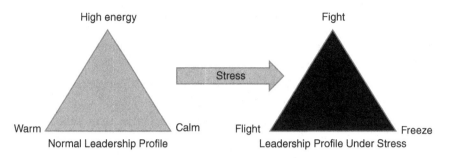

Figure 7.1 How stress affects leadership style.

Institute has done some interesting work on how extreme stress affects leadership style (Sandler, 2012).

In Figure 7.1, the triangle on the left shows three common leadership styles. At the top, you have high-energy, charismatic leaders; on the bottom left, you have warm, inclusive, team-building leaders; and on the bottom right, you have level-headed and analytical leaders. Most people lie somewhere in between these extremes but will prefer one.

When leaders experience severe pressure, they get uneasy and their leadership style changes to that shown in the right-hand triangle. Charismatic leaders go into fight mode and end up being irritable and aggressive. Warm, inclusive leaders go into flight mode and disappear into the team, wanting to be everybody's friend, rather than the boss. Finally, calm, analytical leaders go into freeze mode, shutting their office door and finding it very difficult to decide what needs to be done. Again, these are extreme reactions I'm describing and most people will fall somewhere in between.

Take a few moments to think about Figure 7.1 and where you might be on those triangles.

To reiterate, the biggest factor that protects people from burning out is the ability to switch off from work. Successful people work very hard when they're at work, but when they finish, they can immediately switch their attention to things outside of work, such as family or hobbies. In contrast, a person on the road to burnout will cook a meal or try to get to sleep, but will be still thinking about work. This is the biggest and most robust finding in the literature on avoiding burnout. So have strict boundaries between work and your personal life and try to switch off when you finish.

Chapter takeaways

- Remote working is growing and becoming a routine part of many people's working life.
- Remote working is a positive experience for most people and employers. But it can also increase the risk of burnout.
- People working from home are more productive than office-based employees. This applies to complex, creative tasks, but less so to dull, routine tasks.
- The secret to successful remote working is adapting the workflow to complement the personality. For example, people who are highly extroverted enjoy social contact and people lacking conscientiousness enjoy a lot of structure.
- If you manage a remote team, you need a lot of psychological presence.
- The most effective workflow is to use 'bursty communication': short bursts of intense communication followed by long periods of deep work.
- The big problem with remote working is social isolation and loneliness. Combat this by encouraging online social and work/task interaction.

References

Bloom, N., Liang, J., Roberts, J. & Ying, Z. J. (2015). 'Does Working from Home Work? Evidence from a Chinese Experiment'. *The Quarterly Journal of Economics, 30*(1), 165–218.

Cooperrider, D. L. & Whitney, D. (2005). *Appreciative Inquiry: A Positive Revolution in Change.* San Francisco, Calif.: Berrett-Koehler Publishers Inc.

Dutcher, E. (2012). 'The Effects of Telecommuting on Productivity: An Experimental Examination. The Role of Dull and Creative Tasks'. *Journal of Economic Behavior and Organization, 84*(1), 355–63.

Emerson, R. M. (1971). 'Social Exchange Theory'. *Annual Review of Sociology,* Vol. 2, 335–62.

Holt-Lunstad, J., Smith, T. B. & Layton, J. B. (2010, July). Social Relationships and Mortality Risk: A Meta-analytic Review. *PLoS Medicine, 7*(7). Retrieved from https://doi.org/10.1371/journal.pmed.1000316.

Kahneman, D. (2011). *Thinking, Fast and Slow*. London and New York: Penguin Books.

Kelliher, C. & Anderson, D. (2010). 'Doing More with Less? Flexible Working Practices and the Intensification of Work'. *Human Relations*, 63(1), 83–106.

Larson, B. Z., Vroman, S. R. & Makarius, E. E. (2020). 'A Guide to Managing Your (Newly) Remote Workers'. *Harvard Business Review*, 18 March.

Newport, C. (2016). *Deep Work : Rules for Focused Success in a Distracted World*. London: Piatkus.

Riedl, C. & Woolley, A. W. (2017). 'Teams vs. Crowds: A Field Test of the Relative Contribution of Incentives, Member Ability, and Emergent Collaboration to Crowd-Based Problem Solving Performance'. *Academy of Management Discoveries*, 3(4), 382–403.

Sandler, C. (2012). 'The Emotional Profiles Triangle: Working with Leaders Under Pressure'. *Strategic HR Review*, 11(2), 65–71.

Seligman, M. (2011). *Flourish: A New Understanding of Happiness and Well-Being – and How to Achieve Them*. London: Nicholas Brealey Publishing.

Section 3

ORGANISATION

8

ORGANISATIONAL CULTURE
AND BURNOUT

By far the most important factor that determines whether an individual burns out is the culture of the organisation in which they work. It is the culture that pushes people either towards stress, mental ill-health and burnout, or conversely to psychological safety and high performance. It can feel like the culture exists independently of its individual members. Leaders set the culture, which means an organisation reflects its leaders' values, priorities and emotional intelligence. When the leaders of an organisation understand that burnout can happen all too easily they can take action to minimise the conditions that lead to burnout. These 'anti-burnout' actions will have a direct impact on performance and productivity, then positive change becomes possible.

In this chapter, I will examine the relationship between burnout and organisational culture. I explore the factors that make an organisation's culture good or bad, healthy or toxic. I end the chapter by looking at what actions the leaders of an organisation can take to create a positive, psychologically healthy organisational culture that minimises the risk of burnout.

What is organisational culture?

The famous organisational psychologist Edgar Schein provided the simplest, most helpful and most accepted definition of organisational culture. He wrote,

"Organizational culture is the pattern of basic assumptions that a given group has invented, discovered, or developed in learning to cope with its problems of external adaptation and internal integration, and that have worked well enough to be considered valid, and, therefore, to be taught to new members as the correct way to perceive, think, and feel in relation to those problems." (Schein, 1984)

Schein suggests that this organisational culture exists at three levels:

The observable appearances/artefacts, which people see when they first enter or begin working for a company. They include things like dress code, formality of language and how they organise the space. If you were to wander around the office of a magic circle law firm, it would look very different from what you would see in the office space of an advertising agency. To understand this appearance, we have to consider the next level down, which is the values of the organisation.

We can see the values of an organisation in mission statements and other documents. They often reflect the beliefs of the founder and leaders about how the organisation should be run. These values are what the members of an organisation say, but don't do. Behaviours and practices that can lead to burnout often develop in the space between espoused values and the reality of what happens – between what people say and do. Actual organisational behaviour is more often determined by the basic subjective assumptions of members. Organisational culture is like an iceberg. These first two levels are what you see on the surface. The 90 per cent of the iceberg below the surface (the part that sunk the Titanic) are the basic subjective assumptions held by members of the organisation. These are much harder to see.

The basic subjective assumptions of an organisation develop when particular behaviours prove effective in solving short-term problems and thus become habitual and embedded in the culture. These behaviours (that work) can often contradict the espoused values of an organisation. In such cases, the assumptions almost always win – because at one level, they solve the problem (Schein, 1990). As the well-known organisational consultant Peter Drucker once wrote, "culture eats strategy for breakfast, lunch and dinner" (cited by Schein, 1984).

BOX 8.1 BURNOUT, ORGANISATIONAL CULTURE AND THE MID STAFFS HOSPITAL SCANDAL

A chilling example of organisational culture and the three levels of culture is the Mid Staffordshire hospital scandal. Between January 2005 and March 2009, somewhere between 400 and 1,200 (the figures are disputed) patients died unnecessarily because of poor care at Staffordshire Hospital. This was a small local district general hospital in the rural county of Staffordshire. Evidence presented to the later public inquiry was shocking for its description of the callousness and lack of care afforded to patients. Robert Francis QC chaired the public inquiry and published a report in 2013 in which he cited "a litany of failings in the care of patients". "For many patients the most basic elements of care were neglected," he said. Some patients needing pain relief either got it late or not at all. Others were left unwashed for up to a month. "Food and drinks were left out of the reach of patients and many were forced to rely on family members for help with feeding." Too many patients were sent home before they were ready to go, and ended up back in hospital soon afterwards. "The standards of hygiene were at times awful, with families forced to remove used bandages and dressings from public areas and clean toilets themselves for fear of catching infections." Patients' calls for help to use the toilet were ignored, with the result that they were left in soiled sheets or sitting on commodes for hours "often feeling ashamed and afraid". "Misdiagnosis was common" (Mid Staffordshire NHS Foundation Trust Public Inquiry, 2013).

The Francis Report identified several contributing factors to the Mid Staffs scandal, including poor leadership, chronic staff shortages – especially in nursing – and low morale in support staff. Francis also attributed the underlying problems at Mid Staffs to the decision of the hospital trust's board to reduce Trust spending by £10 million to bolster its bid to achieve foundation trust status. They met this target by cutting staffing levels, which were poor to begin with. This also meant they turned a blind eye to the concerns and complaints from hospital staff.

The Mid Staffs scandal is a classic example of a toxic organisational culture. Had you walked into Staffordshire Hospital in 2005 and looked around, you would have seen an average NHS hospital with doctors and nurses walking about, beds in wards and signs to outpatient departments. You probably would not have seen any direct evidence of neglect or cruelty. This is what Edgar Schein means by the observable appearance or artefacts of an organisation.

(Continued)

Had you read a key document, like the annual report of the Mid Staffordshire NHS Trust, you would have found many commitments to high-quality patient care and probably an inspiring mission statement. These are what Schein would call the organisation's espoused values. If you had spoken to the staff, especially the most senior staff, these are the values they would have parroted to you.

However, as Schein says, what's important in determining organisational culture is the underlying assumptions held by the members of that organisation. The key underlying assumption at Mid Staffs was that saving money took precedence over patient care. This led to a culture of poor performance, cynicism and staff exhaustion – the key components of burnout. In Chapter Five, I described how Isabel Menzies Lyth observed that hospital social systems under pressure create anxiety and feelings of fragmentation for nurses and this often results in failings in care (Menzies, 1960). Burnout was, arguably, one factor that contributed to the appalling tragedy of the Mid Staffs hospital scandal.

How does culture contribute to burnout?

The story of the Mid Staffs hospital scandal perfectly illustrates the relationship between organisational culture, burnout and poor outcomes. One of the main contributing factors to the scandal was the focus on finances rather than the purpose and meaning of healthcare. The literature shows that a focus on simply making money (or, in the case of Mid Staffs, saving money) rather than providing quality and value and taking care of employees leads to high levels of burnout (Belias et. al, 2014; Schaufeli & Baker, 2004).

In their book, *Time, Talent, Energy*, Michael Mankins and Eric Garton (2017) place the responsibility for employee burnout firmly with the organisational culture, not the individual. When they investigated organisations with high rates of burnout, they identified three common factors:

1   Excessive collaboration.
2   Poor time management and boundaries.
3   A tendency to overload the most capable people with too much work.

These three factors destroy the employee's ability to focus on complex tasks, and they sabotage their time away from work, which is necessary for recovery. This inability to switch off at the end of the workday and focus on anything but work is the best predictor of burnout (Leiter et al., 2014). Let's look at these three factors in more depth.

Excessive collaboration

Do you ever get sick of the endless rounds of meetings at work to ensure that everyone is consulted and included in decisions? That is what I mean by excessive collaboration. Most organisations demand collaboration far beyond what they need to get the job done. This results in overloaded diaries and time wasted in meetings, rather than time used productively to get things done.

In one company that Mankins and Garton studied, the average manager lost one day a week responding to emails and two days a week attending meetings. The most talented managers lost even more time to collaboration, because their skills generated more demands on their time, resulting in more responsibility and a larger workload (see 'Overloading of the most capable').

Poor time management and boundaries

In many organisations, the demand for high productivity has significantly outpaced the development of organisational processes and structures to support this demand. Most of the time, employees have to work out as best they can how to manage their time and workload in order to get things done and minimise stress and the increasing danger of burnout. Most have limited ability to fight an organisational culture where overwork is seen as normal and is actively rewarded.

Overloading of the most capable

"If you want a job done, give it to the busiest person," so the saying goes. Employee workloads have increased, usually without a commensurate increase in staff numbers. As a result, managers often overestimate how much can be accomplished by employees who feel constantly under pressure and who usually end up working unpaid hours by staying late or taking work home. The best people, and those whose knowledge and skills are most in demand, become the biggest victims of overload.

Daily burnout experiences

Burnout isn't a black-and-white or on-and-off experience. Researchers have found that there is considerable variation between people (some people burn out more easily than others) and in individuals prone to and suffering with burnout. A person suffering with burnout might feel okay for much of the day and only start to feel burnt out at distinct points in the day (Leiter et al., 2014).

Daniel Beale and Howard Weiss have suggested that life at work is really a series of episodes and that people's experiences, including their experiences that lead to burnout, make up these episodes. They explored how people felt about specific episodes that occurred at work. Did the episode make them feel good or bad, happy or sad, energised or tired? Then the researchers looked at what people did in response to the specific events. The important thing they found related, unsurprisingly, to how successfully the individuals could recover after work. They learned that if we expose a person to what they call daily burnout experiences and they can go home and recover, then the following day that person is more resilient at dealing with those burnout experiences. If, however, the person goes home and cannot relax and recover, that just adds to the accumulation of burnout experiences and compounds the burnout (Beal & Weiss, 2013).

These individual daily burnout experiences, resulting in exhaustion, cynicism and reduced performance, all depend on moment-to-moment events in the working day. This model explains well why negative (and indeed positive) feelings at work fluctuate in most people. Other researchers have found that it is not so much the absence of positive events at work that leads to burnout but rather the presence of negative events. Positive events (for example, a customer expressing gratitude) only seem to benefit workers when there has been a significant build-up of negative events. On a normal day with a few negative events, positive events don't seem to affect their level of fatigue (Gross et al., 2011).

Let's imagine for a moment an average employee called John. John has lots of daily events at work, some of which are positive and some negative. Let's assume that John works in an organisation that is poor at managing stress. Consequently, John is under constant pressure. After a while, John's negative daily events become daily burnout experiences. The research suggests that the key factor that will either dissipate these daily burnout experiences or exacerbate them is how well John can switch off and recover after work. If his recovery is successful, then he is better able to manage the daily burnout experiences the following day. If John isn't able to recover – if he takes home work, worries and remains preoccupied with work – then his stress and anxiety will accumulate and compound, making the daily burnout experiences the following day even more difficult to manage. This circular process will eventually lead to burnout and breakdown. Xanthopoulou and Meier (2014) explain this process in more detail.

How to change a high-risk burnout culture into an anti-burnout culture

In their classic book on organisational culture change, Roger Connors and Tom Smith (2012) describe an organisation as a pyramid. At the top of the pyramid there are *results*. These results are the products or services that the organisation delivers, and they can be good or bad in terms of quality and/ or profitability. At the next level down are the *actions that produce the results*. This is the 'work', what you would see if you wandered around the organisation. Using the iceberg metaphor again, these are the two levels above the water that you can see.

Underpinning and driving those actions are the *beliefs of people working in the organisation* (what Schein describes as the underlying assumptions). Finally, at the base of the pyramid are *people's daily experiences at work*. It is these daily experiences that really determine people's beliefs. Employees in an organisation take a lot more notice of what they can see, what tangibly happens to them; rather than what leaders and managers say or the contents of an organisational mission statement. It is these day-to-day experiences that result either in a high-performance workplace or a workplace characterised by burnout and poor performance.

Connors and Smith argue that in order to change the results, leaders have to look at each level of this pyramid, starting at the base with people's daily experiences. This model connects nicely with the research on burnout. If we can change people's daily burnout experiences to daily, energising experiences; then that would be a good foundation for an anti-burnout culture. In the rest of this chapter, I will discuss some ways to achieve this.

Step 1: develop a culture of psychological safety

Amy Edmondson writes that a sense of psychological safety is the essential characteristic of a high-performance organisational culture (Edmondson, 2019). Conversely, a lack of psychological safety results in a toxic organisation. She describes a culture of psychological safety as one in which people feel they can speak up, express their concerns and be heard. In a psychologically safe workplace, people are not full of fear and not trying to cover their tracks to avoid being embarrassed or punished. This is a workplace where people can offer suggestions and take sensible risks without provoking retaliation. Psychological safety was conspicuously lacking at Stafford Hospital, with tragic consequences.

Project Aristotle was the codename of research by Google on why some teams performed better than others. It found that psychological safety was by far the single most important factor driving success. Charles Duhigg, the Pulitzer prize winning author and business journalist, summed it up well, when he wrote:

> Individuals on teams with higher psychological safety are less likely to leave Google, they're more likely to harness the power of diverse ideas from their teammates, they bring in more revenue, and they're rated as effective twice as often by executives.
>
> (Duhigg, 2016)

Creating a culture of psychological safety is difficult and messy and is beyond the scope of this book. However, in his book on cognitive diversity, *Rebel Ideas*, Matthew Syed describes two easy-to-implement techniques that go a long way to creating a sense of psychological safety in an organisation (Syed, 2020).

Brainwriting

Brainwriting is a way of generating creative ideas. It's different from its older sibling brainstorming, because instead of presenting your ideas verbally out loud, you are asked to write them down on cards, which are then posted on a wall for the rest of the group to vote on. This works well for two reasons.

First, everyone gets the chance to contribute (equal contribution is one of the key factors in psychological safety), no matter how shy they might be. This means that the organisation gains access to the thinking of everyone in the team, not just one or two more extroverted, confident people.

The second advantage of brainwriting is that it detaches status and authority from the ideas. The golden rule of brainwriting is that nobody may identify themselves on their idea card – no matter how subtly they might do this. You can't use names, titles or distinctive handwriting (block capitals only, please). Separating the idea from the status of the person who came up with it means that people vote on the quality of the proposal, rather than the status of the person who suggested it. According to Syed:

> When brainwriting is put head to head with brainstorming, it generates twice the volume of ideas, and also produces higher quality ideas when rated by independent assessors. The reason is simple. Brainwriting liberates diversity from the constraints of dominance dynamic.
>
> (Syed, 2020)

Amazon's Golden Silence

For the past ten years or so, Amazon meetings have started with 30 minutes of silence. During this time, people in the meeting read a six-page memo that summarises, in narrative form, the main agenda item. It's important that this is written down properly and not summarised in bullet points. In doing this, the people presenting the ideas must consider them carefully before learning the opinions of others. Thus Amazon's Golden Silence encourages and supports diversity of thinking and a real consideration of the strengths and weaknesses of the ideas, and reduces any risk that the strengths and weaknesses and diverse suggestions will either not get mentioned or will be crushed by the dominance hierarchy that is common in many corporate meetings.

Step 2: reverse-engineer Mankins and Garton's three burnout factors

The three common factors associated with a burnout culture identified by Mankins and Garton (2017) were: excessive collaboration, poor time management/boundaries and a tendency to overload the most capable people with too much work.

Keep meetings to a minimum – and keep them short (excessive collaboration)

Unnecessary meetings burn up time and become an obstacle to getting the work done. Many people don't like meetings because they would rather be getting on with the task at hand. In some organisations, where the work is emotionally difficult, organising excessive meetings is an unconscious tactic to avoid the work.

To tackle this, empower people to make decisions. When you are thinking about your meetings, consider whether they are necessary and whether everybody you are considering inviting actually needs to be there. In the previous chapter, I described how researchers found that short bursts of communication ('bursty communication'), in contrast with traditional ways of communicating, significantly improved the performance of remote-working teams (Riedl & Woolley, 2017). The same principle, I would argue, applies to office-based teams.

Improve workplace time management and boundaries (poor time management and boundaries)

The relationship between poor boundaries and burnout has been a theme throughout this book. Leaders face a constant dilemma between improving performance/output and making sure their employees look after their health by taking breaks and not overworking. Often leadership teams prioritise the former and neglect the latter. This may well be an effective strategy in the short term, but it is a disastrous strategy in the long term. Organisations should proactively and firmly create a culture where work is done in work time, and home is for rest and recuperation (for family, friends, hobbies and interests). Most of the time, the problem is that the senior leadership team is hopeless at doing this themselves. They often have the worst work–life balance of anybody in the organisation. Therefore, senior leadership teams have to set an example and model the very behaviour that they want to see in other people. I think it was Gandhi who said, "be the change you want to see." It's important to be clear when somebody (be it a leader or employee) is at work and not at work.

When the person is at work, it's also important that their time is managed to ensure they do their job as well as they possibly can. This doesn't mean eight hours with their nose to the grindstone. It means working in brief bursts of activity with frequent breaks. There is a lot of advice about this elsewhere in this book.

Take care of your most capable people (overloading of the most capable)

I sometimes do an exercise with the leadership teams I work with. I ask them to make a list of the people in their team. Then I ask them to reflect on why they ordered the list in the way they did. For example, why did they put 'James' at the top of the list rather than at the bottom or somewhere in the middle? The answers are always interesting. Some people order the list based on how long each person has been in the team; others order it depending on how close individuals sit to them. However, most managers put at the top of the list either their 'go-to', most capable people or their 'pain in the backside' people. This exercise can reveal a lot about how these leaders view their teams and work. Those who place the 'difficult' team members at the top of the list can be preoccupied with looking after people and be problem-focused. Those who put their 'go-to' people at the top are often more preoccupied with the task than the well-being of people. This is a simplification, but there is a grain of truth in it.

The Inclusion self-assessment in Table 8.1 is a tool that you can use to understand this process in yourself and how it impacts on your team.

Table 8.1 Inclusion self-assessment

1–10	Knowledge	Communication	Delivery	Team	Development	Being Heard	TOTAL
Team Member (Initials)	Do I take an active interest in them?	How much 'face time' do I have with them?	How likely am I to ask them to deliver an important piece of work?	Do I give them the support they need to play a full part in the team?	Do I give them the support they need to take advantage of development opportunities?	Do I give them the support they need to contribute to and be heard in discussions or in decisions?	
TOTAL							

To use the Inclusion self-assessment, first of all list the members of your team by initial in the first column. Give yourself a score from 1 (low) to 10 (high) for the various categories (for example, 'Do I take an active interest in them?'). Total up the scores along the rows, and then total the scores in the columns. When you have completed this, you will have a score for each team member and a score for each category (knowledge, communication, delivery etc.).

Your total for each team member will give you a rough-and-ready assessment of how much you include each team member in each domain. The category totals will give you a rough indication of how comfortable you are in dealing with people in each of the domains. Every leader I've used this tool with has found it a useful way to reflect not only on how they interact with members of their team, but also on how comfortable they feel with such tasks as communicating and delegating.

Chapter takeaways

- By far the most important factor in burnout is organisational culture.
- Organisational culture is the set of commonly accepted and key assumptions held by members of an organisation.
- In a boxing match between culture and strategy, put your money on culture to win by a knockout, every time.
- Organisational culture contributes to burnout in three ways:
  - Excessive collaboration.
  - Poor time management and boundaries.
  - Overloading the most capable.
- Burnout happens as a result of many daily workplace experiences.
- To minimise burnout, change these daily experiences.
- Psychological safety is a key factor in minimising burnout risk.
- Practical things you can do to minimise burnout include:
  - Keep meetings to a minimum and manage them well.
  - Improve boundaries and time management.
  - Take care of your most capable people.

References

Beal, D. J. & Weiss, H. M. (2013). 'The Episodic Structure of Life at Work'. In A. B. Bakker & K. Daniels (Eds.), *A Day in the Life of a Happy Worker (Current Issues in Work and Organizational Psychology)*, pp. 8–24. New York: The Psychology Press.

Belias, D., Dimitrios, B. & Konstantinos, V. (2014). 'Organisational Culture and Job Burnout – A Review'. *IMPACT: International Journal of Research in Business Management*, 2(1), 43–62.

Connors, R. & Smith, T. (2012). *Change the Culture, Change the Game: The Breakthrough Strategy for Energizing Your Organization and Creating Accountability for Results*. New York: Portfolio/Penguin.

Duhigg, C. (2016). 'What Google Learned From Its Quest to Build the Perfect Team'. *New York Times Sunday Magazine*, 16 February, p. 20. Retrieved from https://www.nytimes.com/2016/02/28/magazine/what-google-learned-from-its-quest-to-build-the-perfect-team.html.

Edmondson, A. C. (2019). *The Fearless Organization: Creating Psychological Safety in the Workplace for Learning, Innovation, and Growth*. Hoboken: Wiley.

Gross, S., Semmer, N. K., Meier, L. L., Kälin, W., Jacobshagen, N., & Tschan, F. (2011). 'The Effect of Positive Events at Work on After-work Fatigue: They Matter Most in Face of Adversity'. *Journal of Applied Psychology*, 96(3), 654–64.

Leiter, M. P., Bakker, A. B. & Maslach, C. (eds) (2014). *Burnout at Work: A Psychological Perspective (Current Issues in Work and Organizational Psychology)*. New York: Psychology Press.

Mankins, M. C. & Garton, E. (2017). *Time, Talent, Energy: Overcome Organizational Drag and Unleash Your Team's Productive Power*. Brighton, Massachusetts: Harvard Business Review Press.

Menzies, I. E. P. (1960). 'A Case-Study in the Functioning of Social Systems as a Defence against Anxiety'. *Human Relations*, 13(2), 95–121.

Mid Staffordshire NHS Foundation Trust Public Inquiry (2013). *Report of the Mid Staffordshire NHS Foundation Trust Public Inquiry*. Retrieved from: https://assets.publishing.service.gov.uk/government/uploads/system/uploads/attachment_data/file/279124/0947.pdf.

Riedl, C. & Woolley, A. W. (2017). 'Teams vs. Crowds: A Field Test of the Relative Contribution of Incentives, Member Ability, and Emergent Collaboration to Crowd-Based Problem Solving Performance'. *Academy of Management Discoveries*, 3(4), 382–403.

Schaufeli, W. & Baker, A. (2004). 'Job Demands, Job Resources and Their Relationship with Burnout and Engagement: A Multi-sample Study'. *Journal of Organizational Behavior*, 25, 293–315.

Schein, E. H. (1984). 'Coming to a New Awareness of Organizational Culture'. *MIT Sloan Management Review*, Winter. Retrieved from: https://sloanreview. mit.edu/article/coming-to-a-new-awareness-of-organizational-culture/.

Schein, E. H. (1990). 'Organizational Culture'. *American Psychologist*, 45(2), 109–19.

Schein, E. H. (1991). 'What Is Culture?' In S. M. P. Frost (Ed.), *Reframing Organizational Culture*, pp. 243–53. London and New York: Sage.

Syed, M. (2020). *Rebel Ideas: The Power of Diverse Thinking*. London: John Murray.

Xanthopoulou, D. & Meier, L. L. (2014). 'Daily Burnout Experiences: Critical Events and Measurement Challenges'. In M. P. Leiter, A. B. Bakker & C. Maslach (Eds.), *Burnout at Work: A Psychological Perspective (Current Issues in Work and Organizational Psychology)*, pp. 80–101. Hove: Psychology Press.

9

LEADERSHIP AND BURNOUT

This chapter is about how leadership style affects burnout in organisations. It's also about how burnt-out leaders can either make everyone else's life hell or just collapse. Most of us can think of bosses who have been a nightmare to work for:

- The Type A tyrants who were workaholics and expected everyone else to be the same.
- The dithering, indecisive, laissez-faire bosses who couldn't make a decision to save their life.
- The nasty, manipulative, 'kiss up and kick down' psychopathic types.

Some of us will also have stories of great bosses, the sort of bosses that you would move mountains for. Bosses who would fight for the time and resources that you needed to do a good job. The kind, supportive bosses whom you always felt able to talk to, and the positive bosses who always made a point of saying thank you when you'd done a good job.

In this chapter, I discuss three of the dominant leadership styles: transactional leadership, transformational leadership and destructive leadership.

For the last category, I consider the Dark Triad – where psychopathy meets management theory. I then look at the literature on leadership style and burnout, and figure out which leadership style minimises the risk of burnout.

It's important to understand the role leadership plays in burnout for two reasons. Firstly, the leaders of an organisation determine its culture; in Chapter 8, I explain how the most important factor affecting burnout is organisational culture. Secondly, the relationship between the individual employee and their immediate line manager plays a massive role in that employee's well-being. It is the line manager who often determines whether the employee has a reasonable workload, takes proper rest breaks, and feels motivated and engaged. This relationship between leaders (at whatever level) and members of an organisation is primary in determining the well-being of members of the organisation. Leadership has a profound impact on culture and burnout.

What is leadership?

Most people think of leadership in organisations as being a bit like the traditional organisational chart, with the CEO at the top followed by layers of managers below, as in Figure 9.1. This is a typical hierarchical model of leadership. Here, two directors are responsible to the CEO and manage people in their function in the organisation.

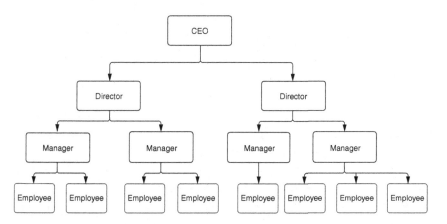

Figure 9.1 A hierarchical model of leadership.

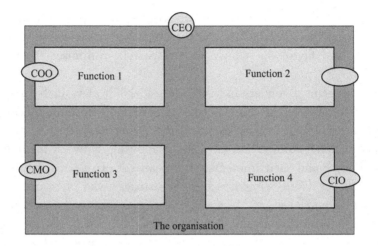

Figure 9.2   A systemic model of leadership.

A different way of thinking about leadership would be to see the leader straddling the boundary between the function that they manage and the organisation as a whole. This is a systemic model of leadership (Roberts, 2019).

In this way of thinking about leadership relationships, the CEO straddles the boundary between the organisation and the outside world. A CEO needs to know what's going on inside the organisation as well as having a good awareness of how things are developing in the outside world. Inside the organisation, you might have a chief operations officer (COO) managing the operations function but also knowing the strategy and tactics of the whole organisation. Figure 9.2 illustrates this way of representing leadership in an organisation.

Problems can arise when the leader loses their boundary position and either gets sucked into their team or pulled away from their team into the wider organisation. In Figure 9.2, the chief marketing officer (CMO) might spend most of their time in management meetings or perhaps with external suppliers like advertising agencies. When they do this, they neglect the people in the marketing team. Those they manage end up feeling neglected and think their manager is only interested in 'swanning off with the rest of the leadership team or drinking white wine with the admen'. Conversely, the chief information officer (CIO) might well spend most of their time working in the IT team and not pay much attention to senior management and strategic responsibilities. In this case, the person's colleagues in the senior leadership team, and the CEO, may regard them as not having much leadership capability because they avoid taking strategic decisions and responsibility for the organisation as a whole.

If you think back to the Mid Staffs example in Chapter 8, the managers there were too concerned with issues on the outside of their boundary. They were concerned with meeting targets and saving money, and ignored the issues inside the boundary involving day-to-day patient care and so on. The staff at Staffordshire Hospital would have been suffering with high levels of compassion fatigue, cynicism and exhaustion. In turn this would have resulted in very poor performance. In other words, many of the staff at Staffordshire Hospital were burnt-out, and the signs of burnout were either missed or ignored by the leadership (who may themselves have experienced burnout). This is an example of the link between leadership style and burnout.

In our careers, many of us will have come across leaders who were hardly ever seen because they were always away 'at meetings' or, as many staff might say, "hobnobbing with the bigwigs". Similarly, we can all think of leaders who were just too enmeshed with their team. They were more interested in wanting to be everybody's friend than taking up their authority as a leader. Every leader will, from time to time, get pulled into the team or pulled away from the team, but to do the job properly, it's important to straddle the boundary between the inside of your department and the organisation as a whole, and the outside world.

Neither of these models is right or wrong, but the 'leadership at the boundary' model helps us think about leadership behaviour in the real-life context of an organisation. It is particularly helpful in thinking about burnout. Is the leader spending too much time away from those they manage and neglecting them? Or, conversely, is the leader micromanaging and spending too much time within the team, and neglecting their role as senior leader and their ability to influence the culture and perhaps resources available to their team?

Within the hierarchical or boundaries framework, you will encounter leaders using a number of leadership styles. The leadership styles that you are most likely to come across and easily identify are transactional leadership, transformational leadership and destructive leadership, as outlined in the following sections.

Transactional leadership

Transactional leadership is based on the psychological theory of behaviourism. This means, put very simply: reward the behaviour you want to see and punish the behaviour you don't want to see. It is the management style that you are most likely to find in day-to-day workplace encounters. Many organisations claim to have a transformational leadership culture (see the next section), but in practice most use the traditional transactional model.

As the name implies, the underlying assumption of transactional leadership is that work is based on a series of transactions. Relationships within an organisation are seen as simply transactions, where employees exchange time and skills with the employer for money. A transactional leader rewards good performance with an increase in pay or promotion. Conversely, poor performance is 'punished' or sanctioned by means of the performance management structure.

Although transactional leadership is seen by some as rigid, old-fashioned and not very progressive, it does have some advantages. In most transactional leadership cultures the boundaries are clear. People know where they stand. This clarity around boundaries provides members of the organisation with a sense of security and stability, since work and the behaviour of managers is generally predictable. This approach can work well in some types of highly structured organisations such as the military. It also works well in times of crisis, when decisions have to be made quickly and it's helpful to know who is in charge.

However, this approach to leadership can be stifling. Most people come to work for lots of reasons other than just the money, and a transactional leadership style can get in the way of the more intrinsic rewards for work. That is because transactional leaders have two possible responses to employee efforts: reward them with money, praise or time off, or sanction them. This is quite a restricted range of responses that can alienate the employee from the meaning of their work. It reinforces and rewards the notion that people only work for the money. This attitude smothers intrinsic motivation and discretionary effort, and can inspire the cynicism we see in burnout. To counter this problem in transactional leadership, management theorists came up with the notion of transformational leadership.

Transformational leadership

In 1973, the psychologist James Downton coined the phrase 'transformational leadership'. The idea arose following his research on charisma in organisations (Downton, 1973). In this research he identified the importance of being able to inspire people in leadership. The concept of transformational leadership was further developed by Bernard Bass. He described the four personality characteristics of leadership that inspire achievement and success (Bass, 1985). He called these:

- *Idealised influence*: essentially, this means setting a good example and being a role model, but with knobs on. Idealised influence is a mixture of charisma, credibility and warmth.
- *Inspirational motivation*: this is the ability of the leader to inspire other people to take action. It doesn't necessarily require charisma, but members of the organisation do need to perceive high levels of integrity and values in the leader. The leader must communicate a strong vision.
- *Intellectual stimulation*: good leaders constantly challenge and stimulate members of an organisation to move forward and do better. Leaders who are able to demonstrate intellectual stimulation make sure that those they manage are never bored. They are good at pushing people to their limits, but not pushing them so far they become stressed or burnt-out.
- *Individualised consideration*: leaders demonstrate high levels of individualised consideration when they show a genuine concern for the well-being of those they lead. They know people's names, and often the names of their families. They are good at spotting when a member of staff might be struggling, and at having the confidence to step in and help. They inspire loyalty, commitment and discretionary effort.

A great example of transformational leadership is Winston Churchill during World War II. Churchill was a charismatic speaker and had high levels of credibility with the British public during the Second World War. He didn't just tell people what to do, but inspired them. He had a strong and unwavering vision and frequently reminded people of the meaning of the war: to preserve freedom, rather than just defeat Germany. Finally, he demonstrated a very high level of caring by spending much time visiting people sheltering from the bombs in Tube stations as well as visiting troops deployed in the theatre of war. In other words, Churchill's leadership wasn't merely transactional. He went far beyond telling people what to do and promising rewards, for a successful outcome.

Destructive leadership

There are two very different types of destructive leadership: passive (laissez-faire) leadership and aggressive (bullying) leadership.

- Passive (laissez-faire) leaders are those who avoid or delay making decisions and taking action when problems arise. They also have poor relationships with those they manage because they tend not to praise good behaviour or admonish poor behaviour. Passive leaders are terrified of conflict and will do everything they possibly can to avoid it. Passive leadership causes all kinds of problems, such as role confusion, with people not being sure what is expected of them. Passive leadership also causes bad feelings when employees who behave badly or 'freeload' are tolerated. This confusion and lack of perceived fairness causes enormous levels of stress in members of the organisation.
- Aggressive leaders are the 'Type A' personalities described in Chapter 4. They are usually the people at the top of the organisational dominance hierarchy. They achieve dominance by being assertive, loud and forceful in their interactions with others and by using coercion and intimidation to get their way. Essentially, they are bullies.

The Dark Triad

Of the aggressive leaders, the most damaging are those who have Dark Triad personality traits. In 2002, Delroy Paulhus and Kevin Williams wrote a classic paper identifying the three personality traits that are the cause of most problems in organisations, especially when people with these traits occupy positions of leadership. They termed this 'the Dark Triad' (Paulhus & Williams, 2002).

The Dark Triad consists of three traits: Machiavellianism, narcissism and psychopathy. Leaders with this Dark Triad of personality are amoral, cynical and manipulative. They have an exaggerated sense of entitlement and feel superior to other people. They genuinely don't care about others and they are impulsive. In the big five model of personality, these are highly extroverted individuals who are low on agreeableness, openness and neuroticism. In other words, they are loud, enjoy combat and don't worry about anything.

The novelist John le Carré described the Dark Triad personality beautifully in his 2014 novel, *A Delicate Truth*. One of the characters, Jay Crispin, is described as "your normal, rootless, amoral, plausible, half-educated, nicely spoken frozen adolescent in a bespoke suit, with an unappeasable craving for money, power and respect, regardless of where he got them from" (le Carré, 2014, p. 295).

Psychopaths in the workplace

Of the three personality traits making up the Dark Triad, the most malevolent is psychopathy. An interesting study by Clive Boddy of a sample of 346 Australian senior white collar workers found that around 26 per cent of workplace bullying is accounted for by the 1 per cent of employees who are corporate psychopaths (Boddy, 2011).

When most people hear the word 'psychopath', they think of serial killers like Fred and Rosemary West or fictional characters like Hannibal Lecter. However, these violent killers are just the tip of the iceberg. The world's leading expert on psychopaths, Professor Robert Hare, has estimated that only one in thirty thousand psychopaths goes on to kill or commit serious violence (Hare, 1994). Like the bulk of the iceberg, most psychopaths exist unseen and out of sight beneath the waterline. And like the iceberg that sank the *Titanic*, they can cause massive damage to businesses and those who work in them.

Psychopathy exists on a continuum. Most psychopaths aren't physically violent, and, interestingly, most violent people aren't psychopaths. The majority of psychopaths stay within the confines of the law (sometimes only just). Psychopaths make up about 1 per cent of the general population. The figure rises to 4 per cent in corporate executives (Hare, 1994). This figure is higher because the psychopath's ruthlessness, ability to manipulate people and glib charm helps them to quickly climb the corporate ladder.

So, if your business employs 100 people, it's likely there will be between one and four psychopaths walking around the building, probably in positions of influence or authority. You can also guarantee that these people will cause most of the problems in the business.

What is a psychopath?

In 1977, Harvard psychologist Cathy Widom placed an advert in a local newspaper. It read: "Wanted: charming, aggressive, carefree people who are impulsively irresponsible but are good at handling people and looking after number one." This was how she found subjects for her classic study on 'non-institutionalised psychopaths' (Widom, 1977). As she predicted, all of those who responded met the diagnostic criteria for psychopathy. The description used in the advert paints a pretty good picture of how a corporate psychopath might come across in real life.

Psychopaths are people who are superficially normal and often like-able; like the people described in Cathy Widom's advert ("charming, aggressive, carefree people who are impulsively irresponsible but are good at handling people and looking after number one.") However, under this mask of normality they lack any significant emotional life. They don't feel guilt, empathy or anxiety. The only emotions they do experience are a desire to win and rage when they are obstructed or frustrated. This lack of emotions leads to poor impulse control and a lack of respect for other people.

The main factor that determines whether a person with a psychopathic personality ends up in prison or the boardroom seems to be their ability to control their impulsive behaviour and social anxiety. They care about what some people (not all) think of them, which seems to keep them from breaking the law or behaving too impulsively when they know they are being watched (Fowles & Dindo, 2009).

Psychopaths at work

Even murderous psychopaths have to earn a living. Look at these examples:

- Harold Shipman, GP: killed about 250 people.
- Denis Neilson, civil servant: killed 17 men.
- Fred West, builder: killed about 13 women.
- Ted Bundy, lawyer: killed 36 women.

The point is, that even the very worst psychopath, the serial killer, the 1 per cent of the 1 per cent, doesn't look crazy. If you had been one of Dr Shipman's patients, would you, for even a second, have suspected that he was a psychopath and a serial killer? Probably not. They live and work amongst us and are invisible. That is, until they get caught doing something egregiously wrong. That might be killing someone; but more likely, it's lying or embezzling – or bullying a subordinate to such an extent that the victim experiences burnout. Either way, people and businesses are hurt. Psychologists Paul Babiak and Bob Hare have written extensively about psychopaths in the workplace – or corporate psychopaths as they call them (Babiak & Hare, 2006).

Destructive leadership and burnout

It's easy to see that the destructive leadership style of the Dark Triad results in a toxic organisational culture and ultimately burnout for members of that organisation. Dark Triad leaders are abusive and often aggressive, and research shows a strong relationship between this abusive leadership and the factors that result in burnout (Tepper, 2000). Dark Triad leaders leave their direct reports feeling confused, emotionally exhausted, helpless and alienated from the organisation, and experiencing poor work satisfaction (Ashforth, 1997).

The opposite of Dark Triad leadership, passive leadership, is problematic too. These are the leaders who avoid making decisions and taking responsibility, and generally fail to take up any authority. This leads to all kinds of problems, including role confusion and a leadership vacuum, resulting in office politics and power struggles. A study looking at passive leadership in the nursing profession found that it resulted in more burnout, particularly feelings of exhaustion and a lack of professional accomplishment (Kanste et al., 2007). Other research has demonstrated a link between passive leadership and burnout in the IT industry (Hetland et al., 2007).

Ultimately, both aggressive, bullying leadership and absent leadership result in elevated levels of burnout.

Anti-burnout leadership

If Dark Triad leadership results in burnout, then the model that minimises the risk of burnout is transformational leadership. (Although in a highly structured organisation, or when an organisation is going through a crisis, transactional leadership may work best.) When employees feel supported, they are far less likely to suffer the symptoms of burnout – and this applies to all three domains of burnout (cynicism, exhaustion and poor performance). Research by Raymond Lee and Blake Ashforth found that supervisory support when compared with peer support was highly effective in minimising burnout, especially emotional exhaustion (Lee & Ashforth, 1996).

It's all very well having a supportive and sympathetic boss, but if you are overwhelmed by the amount and demands of your work, you are still likely to experience some burnout symptoms. However, the evidence says that even in the face of chronic work demands, supportive leadership and supervision will act as a buffer to minimise burnout (Bakker et al., 2005).

Rittschof and Fortunato (2016) looked at the relationship between burnout and transformational leadership in a group of 197 child-protection professionals. Child protection is an extremely stressful and emotionally demanding occupation by anyone's standards. The researchers pointed out that it has a burnout rate of somewhere between 20 and 40 per cent. They found that transformational leadership significantly minimised the risk of burnout.

Does transformational leadership suit everyone? This was the question addressed by Kristin Hildebrand and colleagues, who wondered whether transformational leadership was good at minimising the effects of burnout in employees who were more open to experience (high on the openness factor in the big five personality model). To me, this idea makes sense, because if you are a person who is low on openness – in other words, a conservative person who hates change and enjoys structure and being told what to do – then having a very transformational leader might actually make you more stressed. In fact, this proved to be the case, with employees who were open to experience benefiting most from transformational leadership. The researchers concluded that transformational leadership is effective in reducing burnout, but employee personality needs to be taken into account (Hildebrand et al., 2018).

Transformational leadership helps members of an organisation connect with the meaning and purpose of what they're doing, and it emphasises the importance of actively demonstrating genuine concern and responsibility for members of the organisation. On the face of it, then, transformational leadership seems to be the way to go if you want to minimise the risk of burnout in your organisation. And indeed this is what the research says.

The personal qualities of an anti-burnout leader

Anti-burnout leadership requires you to develop a good awareness of three factors: yourself, other people and the existence of the system that binds you and others together. It also requires the courage to act on that knowledge.

Self-awareness

To lead others in a way that minimises burnout in them, you first have to be aware of burnout symptoms in yourself. Are you feeling more tired than usual? Are you finding yourself feeling more cynical about work and the organisation? Is your performance worse than usual? If you notice any of these experiences in yourself, you should stop, reflect on why you feel as you do, and do something to reverse your own drift to burnout. As the cabin attendant on an aircraft might say, "Put on your own oxygen mask first, before attempting to help others."

Awareness of others

Take a moment and look around at the people you work with. Do they look okay, or do they seem exhausted? Listen to them. Do they sound cynical or sarcastic? Is the workplace banter cruel or disrespectful? In a high-pressure environment where you, as the leader, are feeling overwhelmed, there is more often than not a temptation to keep your head down and become very task-focused rather than people-focused. Remember the bystander effect and the story of Kitty Genovese (see Chapter 4).

Systemic awareness

Always try to keep in mind that you and those you lead are part of the wider organisational system and culture. Are you occupying a place on the boundary of your area of responsibility and the organisation as a whole? Do you know the people in your part of the organisation? Do you have a good awareness of other parts of the organisation, as well as the political and economic context of the organisation as a whole? This is very important because the emergence of burnout is influenced as much by the systemic context as by individual personality. Burnout is greater when an organisation is struggling and under pressure than when it is doing well. Remember the examples of Orange/France Télécom (Chapter 1) and Staffordshire Hospital (Chapter 8).

This awareness is the foundation for creating a culture of psychological safety that minimises the risk of burnout in your workplace.

Chapter takeaways

- Leadership is one of the most important factors in minimising burnout.
- There are two ways of thinking about leadership: leadership as a hierarchy and leadership on the boundary.
- There are three main leadership styles: transactional, transformational and destructive.
- Many destructive leaders have Dark Triad or psychopathic personalities.
- Passive leadership also results in high levels of burnout.
- Transformational leadership minimises burnout, although transactional leadership is also effective in times of crisis.
- Anti-burnout leadership requires a good degree of self-awareness, awareness of others and systemic awareness.

References

Ashforth, B. E. (1997). 'Petty Tyranny in Organizations: A Preliminary Examination of Antecedents and Consequences'. *Canadian Journal of Administrative Sciences*, 14(2), 126–40. Retrieved from https://doi.org/10.1111/j.1936-4490.1997.tb00124.x.

Babiak, P. & Hare, R. D. (2006). *Snakes in Suits: When Psychopaths Go to Work* (1st ed.). New York: HarperCollins.

Bakker, A. B., Demerouti, E. & Euwema, M. C. (2005). 'Job Resources Buffer the Impact of Job Demands on Burnout'. *Journal of Occupational Health Psychology*, 10(2), 170–80.

Bass, B. M. (1985). *Leadership and Performance Beyond Expectation*. New York: Free Press.

Boddy, C. (2011). 'Corporate Psychopaths, Bullying and Unfair Supervision in the Workplace'. *Journal of Business Ethics, 100*(3), 367–79.

Downton, J. V. (1973). *Rebel Leadership: Commitment and Charisma in the Revolutionary Process*. New York: Free Press.

Fowles, D. C. & Dindo, L. (2009). 'Temperament and Psychopathy: A Dual-Pathway Model'. *Current Directions in Psychological Science, 18*(3), 179–83.

Hare, R. D. (1994). 'Predators: The Disturbing World of the Psychopaths among Us'. *Psychology Today, 27*(1), 54–61.

Hetland, H., Sandal, G. M. & Johnsen, T. B. (2007). 'Burnout in the Information Technology Sector: Does Leadership Matter?' *European Journal of Work and Organizational Psychology, 16*(1), 58–75.

Hildebrand, K., Sacramento, C. A. & Binnewies, C. (2018). 'Transformational Leadership and Burnout: The Role of Thriving and Followers' Openness to Experience'. *Journal of Occupational Health Psychology, 23*(1), 31–43.

Kanste, O., Kyngas, H. & Nikkila J. (2007). 'The Relationship between Multidimensional Leadership and Burnout among Nursing Staff'. *Journal of Nursing Management, 15*(7), 731–39.

Lee, T. & Ashforth, B. E. (1996). 'A Meta-analytic Examination of the Correlates of the Three Dimensions of Job Burnout'. *Journal of Applied Psychology, 81*(2), 123–33.

le Carré, J. (2014). *A Delicate Truth* (p. 295). London: Penguin.

Paulhus, D. L. & Williams, K. M. (2002). 'The Dark Triad of Personality: Narcissism,

Machiavellianism, and Psychopathy'. *Journal of Research in Personality, 36*, 556–63.

Rittschof, K. R. & Fortunato, V. J. (2016). 'The Influence of Transformational Leadership and Job Burnout on Child Protective Services Case Managers' Commitment and Intent to Quit'. *Journal of Social Service Research, 42*(3), 372–85.

Roberts, V. Z. (2019). 'The Organisation of Work: Contributions from Open System Theory'. In A. Obholzer & V. Z. Roberts (Eds.), *The Unconscious at Work: A Tavistock Approach to Making Sense of Organizational Life* (2nd ed.) (pp. 37–48). Abingdon: Routledge.

Tepper, B. J. (2000). 'Consequences of Abusive Supervision'. *Academy of Management Journal*, *43*(2), 178–90. Retrieved from https://doi.org/10.5465/1556375.

Widom, C. S. (1977). 'A Methodology for Studying Noninstitutionalized Psychopaths'. *Journal of Consulting and Clinical Psychology*, *45*(4), 674–83.

10

BURNOUT-PROOFING YOURSELF, YOUR STAFF AND YOUR ORGANISATION

In this book, I've described the research into burnout, how it is caused and how it can be avoided. Along the way, I've offered guidance to help you, as the manager or leader in an organisation, to identify and prevent burnout. In this final chapter, I draw together key points in the book to help you see clearly why you need to combat burnout and how exactly you can do so at individual and organisational levels.

An issue to take seriously

"I've been burning the candle at both ends; I'm pretty burnt-out." This is the kind of comment you hear in organisations, and all too often it's met with little more than, "Yeah, me too." Burnout can be seen as par for the course, rather than a recognised problem. And beneath the exhaustion touched on in the 'pretty burnt-out' comment is a whole host of psychological struggles: cynicism, hopelessness, helplessness, detachment, anxiety. These are psychological issues that are highly damaging to people.

Remember, burnout is classed as an occupational phenomenon, not as a mental illness. It's the direct consequence of a dysfunctional workplace. This isn't about an individual being too weak to cope with the regular demands of work; it's about the person, but also, crucially, their role at work and the culture of the organisation. Burnout is a sign that there are underlying organisational problems – and the organisation needs to address these.

Quite simply, an organisation that's rife with burnout isn't a high-performance organisation. How can people be engaged, energetic, passionate, productive, committed and creative when they're burning out? How can you expect an organisation to thrive when its people are floundering? From poor performance to high levels of sickness and staff turnover, burnout costs organisations a fortune.

So investing time and energy in anti-burnout gives a real boost to the organisation. From the managers on the front line to the leaders in the glass offices, there's a great deal that can be done to minimise the risk of burnout. The first step: take this very damaging issue seriously.

Obstacles to tackling burnout

Before you can really deal with the issue of burnout, you need to be aware of some obstacles in your path. Fear of saying the wrong thing or being intrusive can lead you to hold back when you should help. You may also have unconscious biases that get in the way: the bystander effect (thinking someone else will help so you don't need to act) and confirmation bias (having a belief that someone is fine and filtering out all the evidence that they're not). Your own busy schedule at work may be a hindrance to really noticing how others are doing – or you may, in fact, be burning out yourself. And if you are burning out, you really can't be of much help to others. The single best thing you can do to help your employees is to set a good example by avoiding burnout yourself.

Signs to watch for

We all need a challenge and stimulation at work, or we'd be bored and thus unhappy. But when stress consistently goes beyond the optimal point, performance rapidly drops off and burnout results. How do you spot the people who aren't just under the usual stress, but burning out? Here are the signs to look out for:

- Quality of work declines.
- Takes longer to complete work (concentration poor; anxious need to check and recheck).
- Struggles to complete work – colleagues complain they're not pulling their weight.
- Works unusually long hours (hard to focus, so needs to work extra hours to keep up).
- Arrives late (sleep issues).
- Self-neglect, like poor hygiene or looking disheveled.
- Acts snappy or belligerent.
- Is needy, dependent, clingy; wants constant support.

Keep in mind that personality plays a role in risk of burnout. The Type A personality is much more likely to experience burnout. Type A people are highly competitive, self-critical, impatient, aggressive and bullying.

When you realise that someone is suffering with burnout, the first step is to talk to the person in order to establish what's going on with them and what support they need. Be prepared for the person's defence mechanism kicking in, which may lead to denial or projection or even hostility. Persevere, focusing on the person's behaviour at work, not their psychological state.

Ways to minimise the risk of burnout in people

What can you do as a manager or leader to protect your people from burnout? Think of burnout as a depletion of energy – physical, emotional, mental and spiritual – and look to increase the energy levels in your team.

- **Physical energy**: set clear boundaries around work hours – frown on coming in too early and leaving too late; support people to have a life outside of work. Encourage regular breaks of a decent duration (not two minutes to knock back a coffee). Ideally, these breaks will incorporate some exercise and decent nutrition. Consider whether home-working for part of the week would suit some employees better than being at the office full time (see the section 'Considerations for remote working').

- **Emotional energy**: look to increase the ratio of positive to negative interactions in your team (more "Good job"; less "You made a pig's ear of that"). Set aside time in meetings to discuss successes, rather than just focusing on issues. Build a culture of positivity and appreciation.
- **Mental energy**: encourage your team to organise their day into blocks of time (around 90 minutes) devoted to focused work with minimal distractions, interspersed with breaks.
- **Spiritual energy**: meaning is key to having a sense of well-being. Help people to see how and why their works matters – enable them to get feedback from customers, clients and end users.

Also make sure that people understand their job role. The clearer the boundaries around a job role, the lower the risk of burnout. An individual needs a good understanding of when work begins and ends, and what exactly they are responsible for and accountable for. They also need to know the primary task of the organisation (the thing it has to do in order to survive); frequently, different definitions of the primary task exist and this leads to confusion and conflict.

Considerations for remote working

Working from home has become the norm for many people, especially since the Covid-19 pandemic. Some people suit this way of working very well and are highly productive. Others, however, don't find remote working a good fit with their personality: they struggle with the lack of structure and the social isolation, and this can lead to burnout.

As a manager, you can do the following to promote anti-burnout in your remote workers:

- Encourage a structure to the day: a set start and finish time and prearranged break times.
- Schedule check-ins each day – three is ideal. This way staff know you're psychologically and emotionally present for them. Keep the check-ins

short – small, regular bursts of communication work best, so that people can focus properly on their work and don't experience 'Zoom fatigue'. Make sure you communicate job roles clearly, so that staff know what you expect them to do and how.

- Really up the ante with positive feedback. The distance means you need to 'shout' your appreciation. Build in time in a weekly meeting to share what's gone well that week.
- Do what you can to encourage sociability. There's a whole world of ways in which people can connect online now. Informal chatting during a break isn't irrelevant time-wasting; it builds team cohesion.

Watch out for performance dips or over-dependence, which could indicate a person is struggling with remote working and heading for burnout. If you have concerns, reach out and ask: How are you? Is there anything I can do to help?

An anti-burnout culture

We've seen that a person's personality and their job role can contribute to burnout. But by far the most influential factor in burnout is the organisational culture in which a person works. The culture – the set of commonly accepted assumptions held by members of an organisation – can really get under a person's skin, affecting their feelings and behaviour.

Endless rounds of meetings, normalising and rewarding of working beyond normal hours, overloading capable people with too much work – these hinder an employee's ability to do their job well and to have the rest time they need outside of work in order to stay healthy. Negative daily experiences build into burnout.

Leaders set the organisational culture, and so they can change it, by making changes to people's daily experiences. (This makes a lot more impact than releasing a revised mission statement or making a nice speech, because what really matters to people is what work is like for them from day to day.) Here are some ways to build an anti-burnout culture:

- Make the workplace psychological safe, a place where people aren't afraid to speak up and they know they'll be heard.

- Keep meetings short, and only have them when essential.
- Always promote a healthy work–life balance. Ensure leaders model this.
- Take care not to overload the most capable people.

The leader's role in burnout

Leadership, at whatever level, influences organisational culture and burn-out. Clearly, if a leader is burnt-out – exhausted, cynical, detached, hopeless, helpless – then their staff are going to struggle not to burn out themselves. That's why it's crucially important that leaders understand burnout and do all they can to avoid it.

A leader who avoids burnout can still cause burnout in others, though. In particular, two types of destructive leaders have a detrimental effect on the culture and employees. The passive (laissez-faire) leader avoids actually taking the lead, and this gives rise to power struggles and confusion over roles and responsibilities. The aggressive, Type A personality leaders (among them, a good number of psychopaths) make work a misery for staff, who bear the brunt of their abuse, coercion and manipulation.

The ideal style of leadership is transformational, which encompasses the four I's: idealised influence, inspirational motivation, intellectual stimulation and individualised consideration. These leaders set a great example, they inspire loyalty and commitment, and they genuinely care about their staff. Transactional leadership – based on rewards for good work and sanctions for poor work – can continue to burnout, where people feel cynical that they're only working for money, but it has its place in highly structured organisations such as the military and in times of crisis when an organisation needs a firm hand.

Whatever the style of leadership, it's essential to understand burnout; to recognise it in others (as well as yourself); and to be aware of the wider organisational culture and how it's impacting people's well-being. With this knowledge and understanding, you can take anti-burnout action, building a culture of psychological safety and, consequently, a high-performing organisation. One that people want to work for – yourself included.

INDEX

Note: **Bold** page numbers refer to tables. *Italic* page numbers refer to figures.

Printed in the United States
by Baker & Taylor Publisher Services